The Complete ESL/EFL Resource Book

The Complete ESL/EFL Resource Book

Strategies, Activities, and Units for the Classroom

Jean Maculaitis and Mona Scheraga

National Textbook Company
NTC a division of *NTC Publishing Group* • Lincolnwood, Illinois USA

To ESL teachers and students,
past, present, and future,
and
to our husbands,
John and Murray,
who would love a chance to talk
to us in *any* language

To the teacher:
The blackline masters in this book are designed to be photocopied for classroom use only.

1990 Printing

Published by National Textbook Company, a division of NTC Publishing Group.

Manufactured in the United States of America.
Library of Congress Catalog Card Number: 87-62504

0 ML 9 8 7 6 5 4 3

Contents

Preface

The Complete ESL/EFL Resource Book: Strategies, Activities, and Units for the Classroom is based on privileged years of working with nonnative speakers of English at all age/grade levels. Despite a combined total of over thirty years of teaching ESL students and administrating ESL programs, we continue to be inspired by the energy, creativity, spirit of discovery, and just plain fun generated in the ESL/EFL classroom. We have learned to value and keep those techniques which work well, and to try new techniques, new technologies, new strategies for new people who continue to enrich our lives by their presence in our classes and whose lives we hope to touch in some small way. This is not to say, of course, that it has all been "fun and games." Anyone who has ever taught knows just how tough the classroom can be at times. Nevertheless, teaching and learning have remained genuinely exciting for us, an excitement we wish to share with you by means of this book.

Toward that end, *The Complete ESL/EFL Resource Book* begins by helping new teachers organize the ESL/EFL classroom under a variety of circumstances. It takes you through that first day and well into the term. It introduces you to practical strategies for successfully involving parents in the education of their children.

Those new to ESL/EFL as well as those more-experienced second language professionals will find that *The Complete ESL/EFL Resource Book* presents, among other things, specific information, lesson plans, suggestions, and strategies for various adoptable and adaptable units of study. While the book is thematically connected, ease and flexibility in meeting *your* particular needs have been built in: you can pick and choose from these self-contained strategies, activities, and units in the order that best suits you and your students.

As the Table of Contents indicates, the book has been structured in three clusters: Strategies, Activities, and Units. Sections have been grouped under the cluster we felt represented the dominant focus of that particular section. These clusters are not necessarily mutually exclusive. For example, "Welcome Handbooks" is listed under the Activities cluster, but is also viable as a lesson plan that can be incorporated with the unit titled "Can I Have Your Autograph?" Everyone can benefit from "The School, the Home, the Community," listed in the Strategies cluster. You can generate your own activities from this Strategy.

At the end of *The Complete ESL/EFL Resource Book* are references, resources, and blackline masters. There's even a special unit-evaluation form to help you prepare for "next time." Have fun!

Acknowledgments

This book would not have been possible without Dr. Dody Messerschmidt of San Francisco, who introduced us to each other at a NJTESOL/BE Conference with the prophetic words, "You two have got to meet each other! You have the same energy and enthusiasm. You'll really be able to accomplish great things in the profession." We're still trying, Dody.

To the membership of International TESOL, whose high standards of academic professionalism, exhibited in TESOL publications and at conventions, have been a constant source of inspiration, re-evaluation, and new friendships. We especially miss those TESOL friends who are no longer with us but who touched our lives personally and professionally: Dr. Robert Willis, Dr. Ruth Crymes, Dr. Tom Buckingham, Fred Malkames, Jim Weaver, Shirley Yu, and Pepe Prados, husband of former PRTESOL President, Betty Prados.

To Dr. Ronald Todd, Director of NYU's Bilingual Education Vocational Project: Dr. Harvey Nadler of NYU's TESOL Department; and Kalman Bodnar, Chairperson of the Passaic High School English Department, Passaic, New Jersey, thanks for believing in us and allowing our dreams to become realities in the classroom.

We acknowledge with gratitude the sum total of books read, people met, workshops attended, students, teachers, administrators, and parents who have been a source of both inspiration and perspiration.

Very special thanks to Dr. Gladys Nussenbaum, Director of the Bilingual Education Program at William Paterson College, Wayne, NJ, for her enthusiastic support of our project. Sincere thanks also to Marilyn Snider, an educational and business consultant, for reviewing and critiquing *The Complete ESL/EFL Resource Book* from an NLP perspective. (According to Robert Dilts, a leading NLP researcher, consultant, and the author of several NLP texts, "The name Neuro-Linguistic Programming stands for what we maintain to be the basic process used by all human beings to encode, transfer, guide, and modify behavior.") Also important were the support and encouragement of the 1986–1987 Princeton Master Practitioners and Associate Trainers and Armando Riverol, author and ESL media specialist, who was always available to listen and to suggest.

To that very special brand of people, ESL textbook publishers and their representatives, and to the very special people we've worked with at National Textbook Company, Charlie Liebowitz, Michael Ross, and our model of patience, Becky Rauff, whose suggestions and editing cannot be surpassed, for their kindness, competence, and dedication to ESL/EFL students and teachers around the world, a special debt of gratitude.

Most especially, we thank our families who are so proud and supportive, even if they can't figure out exactly what drives us and why we have so much fun "working."

About the Authors

JEAN D'ARCY MACULAITIS, Ph.D., is the President of MAC Testing and Consulting, Inc., and Career Wise, Inc., Sea Bright, New Jersey, and the author of, among other works, *The Maculaitis Assessment Program* (MAC: K–12). She also teaches ESL testing workshops and bilingual vocational courses at New York University. A former ESL program administrator, she has taught ESL from primary through post-doctoral levels in various types of communities. The writer is a member of the Lay Board of Trustees of Georgian Court College, Lakewood, New Jersey, and a member of the Holy Cross School Board of Education, Rumson, New Jersey. She has delivered keynote and plenary addresses and chaired panels for various professional organizations and TESOL affiliates. In cooperation with Exxon, NCTE, MLA, NABE, TESOL, and other professional groups, she wrote "The Standards for the Preparation and Certification of International Studies Teachers in the United States." Currently, she is studying for her Master Practitioner's Certificate in Neuro-Linguistic Programming. Dr. D'Arcy Maculaitis has been cited as "An Outstanding American Educator" by the National Conference of Christians and Jews, elected to "Who's Who in American Professional and Executive Women," and recently named as "one of the 2,000 most distinguished women in America."

MONA SCHERAGA, M.A., a consultant, author, editor, and teacher trainer, has taught ESL at the high school and adult levels and has done teacher training at various colleges and universities with ESL and with bilingual vocational education teachers. She recently served as Co-Vice Chair of the New Jersey State Bilingual Education Advisory Board and as a member of the New Jersey State Bilingual Education Test Search Committee, whose principal task was to select a test to meet state graduation requirements for nonnative English speakers. She has been called to testify before the New Jersey Commissioner of Education and the New Jersey State Board of Education on behalf of bilingual education students and in support of alternative means of teacher certification. Ms. Scheraga is the recipient of a National Education Association Hilda Maehling Fellowship for developing vocational education materials for nonnative English speakers and of a Princeton University Award for Distinguished Secondary School Teaching.

The authors have worked together in the discipline of second language education for more than a dozen years. They have appeared on several television and radio programs, team-taught, written articles, books, and book reviews, edited award-winning newsletters, and presented numerous workshops and seminars throughout the United States and abroad. Both have held offices in TESOL at the affiliate and international levels. They continue to be actively involved in this and other professional organizations.

Declaration of the Rights of the LEP[1] Child

by Jean D'Arcy Maculaitis and Mona Scheraga

- The right to a free and equal education in *practice* as well as in theory.
- The right to dedicated teachers, administrators, and guidance personnel who are not only properly certified but who also care about *and* like the students with whom they are working.
- The right to properly prepared, unbiased, and appropriate texts, tests, and other educational materials.
- The right to be evaluated with valid and appropriate first and second language tests: (a) that have been specifically designed for the LEP child by qualified and highly trained persons, (b) that are properly administered and promptly scored and interpreted by skilled personnel, and (c) whose scores and their interpretation are readily accessible and comprehensible to test takers and their parents or guardians.
- The right to have *several* valid criteria taken into consideration when making any and all evaluative decisions about children, who shall at all times know when, why, and how they are being tested.
- The right to special education services (including gifted and talented programs), where such services can be documented as being appropriate by properly certified and culturally sensitive bilingual education child study teams.
- The right to a properly lighted, well-ventilated, clean classroom with adequate seating.
- The right to sufficient school supplies, properly maintained school equipment, and a secured storage space for belongings.
- The right not to be denied equal access to school lunch programs, medical services (eye tests, immunizations, and so forth), and other basic needs necessary for a healthy and meaningful participation in school life because of language barriers.
- The right to explore the possibilities and to think positively about participating in professional and business worlds, regardless of native language background or ethnicity.
- The right to have one's feelings of self worth not be "measured" by the quality and/or quantity of one's proficiency in English.
- The right to mutual cultural acceptance and all that this implies.
- The right to be respected for being linguistically and culturally different but equal, that is, the right to be treated as a LEP, not a LEPER.

1 LEP = Limited English Proficient

Introduction

The *I's* have it—and all eyes are on you! It's the first day of school. There are few books to be seen, but many faces watching, waiting, and wanting. So you pull out of your "ESL bag" *The Complete ESL/EFL Resource Book: Strategies, Activities, and Units for the Classroom* and all the *I's* that have brought you into this discipline in the first place: idealism, ingenuity, innovation, inventiveness, integrity, imagination, and intuition.

A certain type of individual becomes an ESL teacher, yet ESL teachers are not all one type. This book is for those ESL professionals who take even the best course of study and make it better with their special flair. That special touch can be many things: it is an innovative and energizing spark given off by teachers in touch with what being an ESL professional is really all about, including the effects of the home, school, community, and international affairs. It is the ingenuity and inventiveness of the new teacher with old books. It is the idealism and imagination of the experienced teacher who nurtures risk-taking in teaching and learning, making "mistakes" on both sides of the desk a positive and natural part of the learning process. It is the new teacher who "suddenly" discovers the ability to create the magic of rapport in the classroom.

There's something for everyone in *The Complete ESL/EFL Resource Book*—for teachers *and* students, from the beginner to the advanced, the "quick study" to the slow learner, the artistic to the organizer, the follower to the leader, the introvert to the extrovert, the fearful to the fearless. This book takes you beyond the "survival skills" mentality of recent decades; it is no longer enough merely to survive. Nonnative English speakers must be given the necessary skills to empower themselves cognitively and culturally. Activities presented in this book have been selected because they are particularly relevant and immediately useful for the learner and the teacher. They can be easily adopted and adapted for the age and language experience of your ESL students. There are blackline masters for easy duplication, exciting how-to projects, and examples guaranteed to simplify and stimulate the teaching/learning experience. We have also included Master 12, "For the Teacher: Unit Evaluation Form," to be used as a tangible, private accounting of the strengths and weaknesses of the units from your experience with them.

We hope we will inspire you to take risks in teaching, to encourage your students to take risks in learning, to share your "mistakes" or "failures" together for mutual learning about yourselves and the new language and culture. By focusing on commonly shared experiences, students come to realize what we have known all along, viz., that we are all learners.

Strategies for the Classroom

c. what problems keep them from attending school regularly;

d. the effects of the mobility factor so prevalent among many of them;

e. family situations where education may necessarily be incidental to economic survival in the new land.

In sum, where students are living and with whom can be as valuable to know as, for example, how to create effective lesson plans. Where do our responsibilities end and/or become an infringement on family rights and privacy? Do we as teachers have the right to "educate" our students' parents to the necessity of sacrificing mobility for the sake of their child's education? How do we best deal with the self-fulfilling prophecy (if you project expectations of failure, then your students will satisfy your expectations, *i.e.,* they will fail) so prevalent in the culture of poverty and, sadly, too often inflicted on "minority" youngsters by well meaning but misinformed teachers and administrators? What facilities are being provided to distinguish between functional illiterates and the learning disabled who have gone undetected in their own countries?

Let's not forget those children who have come here with families who enjoy privileged status economically and educationally. They, too, suffer the strains of cultural shock and the problems of isolation and assimilation for which money is no guarantee of protection in the new environment. How can we best help those highly successful career-oriented people who suddenly find themselves at the bottom of the social, educational, and professional ladder here? The ESL teacher is often the sole instigator in pursuing proper facilities and personnel for determining who has which problems and how to deal with and, in many cases, correct the situations as they exist now.

The plethora of problems is such that we find ourselves functioning not only as teachers, psychologists, sociologists, and guidance counselors, but also as multicultural arbiters, coping with different value systems involving concepts of attendance, punctuality, preparedness, and so forth. While understanding and perhaps believing in a more casual, less pressured approach to life, we have the responsibility to initiate our students into how to succeed in America by *really* trying to be on time, to attend school regularly, to take pride in achievement, to adjust to "here," and so forth. Teachers also have a responsibility to help create good, positive self-images through understanding, to provide opportunity for success and positive reinforcement.

Teachers should be able to "read" the body language of their students, to understand why José appears defensive or what makes Kim smile when her problems seem insurmountable.

(For an excellent discussion of the applications of NLP (neuro-linguistic programming) in education, see Robert Dilts, *Applications of Neuro-Linguistic Programming,* Cupertino, California: Meta Publications, 1983, Section VII, 1–39. See also Sid Jacobson, *Meta-Cation: Prescriptions for Some Ailing Educational Processes,* Cupertino, California: Meta Publications, 1983; and C. Van Nagel, Robert Suidzinski, Edward J. Reese, and Mary Ann Reese, *Mega-Teaching and Learning: Neuro Linguistic Programming Applied to Education, Vol. 1,* Indian Rock Beach, Florida: Southern Institute Press, Inc., 1985. Teachers should utilize at every opportunity similarities and differences in the various cultures of their students.)

Culture in this context and throughout this book implies:

High Culture: the self-conscious production of professionals in the arts and humanities. Examples of high culture include literature, painting, architecture, drama, cinema, sculpture, and most forms of music, dance, fashion design, and the other arts.

Folk Culture: the self-conscious productions of nonprofessionals, that is, of people in all walks of life; it takes in a wide variety of artifacts, rule-governed events, and explicit social expectations. In a word, folk culture is the consciously traditional. Examples include oral tradition, religious rites, folk dancing, popular songs, national dishes, superstitions, rules of etiquette, sports and games, holidays, modes of hospitality, courtship practices, treatment of the dependent, body care and adornment, rites of passage, and so forth.

Deep Culture: the largely intangible and out-of-awareness ways in which people from a given region think, feel, and behave in human interactions. The term "out-of-awareness" suggests that implicit and rarely examined assumptions and expectations govern most of what we do in our daily lives. Examples of deep culture include preferred modes of learning, notions of modesty, conceptions of the ideal spouse, patterns of superior/subordinate relations, notions about the value of labor, the conception of the self, the arrangement of physical space, notions about adolescence, the nature of friendship, approaches to problem-solving, nonverbal behaviors of all kinds, and much, much more. [This is the reference applicable above.]

For further information on the teaching of culture, see Dell Hymes, *Language in Culture and Society: A Reader in Linguistics and Anthropology,* New York: Harper and Row Publishers, 1964; Ned H. Seelye, *Teaching Culture: Strategies for Foreign Language Educators,* Lincolnwood, Illinois: National Textbook Company, 1975; and Gloria Grant, ed., *In Praise of Diversity: Multicultural Classroom Applications,* Omaha, Nebraska: Teacher Corps, Center for Urban Education, 1977.

Our personal belief is that ESL teachers should play an intermediary role between their students and other members of the school: faculty, administration, other students, and so forth. Too many hostilities breed on the ignorance of each group about the other's ways.

One of the dilemmas facing ESL teachers is what limits they should observe in encouraging children to pursue a career or college or vocational school education which might be alien to the culture or plans of their parents and might cause conflict at home. Ideally, teachers, parents, and students should work together. Realistically, values and priorities enter the scene again. What is "success"? By whose standards? How do parents surmount their own language obstacles to communicate effectively in an alien culture? How do they change from passive to active roles in the new environment? How quickly can they convert from preconceived notions of their roles in relation to their children's education, when all too often their battle for economic and familial survival supersedes all else? Are they really uninterested in their children's education, as their lack of active participation would lead some to believe, or do economic and personal pressures or cultural traditions necessarily come first? And how can the ESL teacher, the school, and the community be of service here? (See "The School, the Home, the Community" and "Appendix A.")

Like you, we are concerned with the public's apparent lack of sensitivity and understanding of what is involved in being transported to a culture that can be so different in its priorities, attitudes, and customs. We can talk about our ancestors and the "good old days," but the human suffering, school dropout rate, and general lack of self esteem accompanying immigrant populations as they faced scorn and rejection by older "immigrants" turned "Americans" are underscored in available literature and statistics. (See Colin, Greer, *The Great School Legend,* New York: Basic Books, Inc., 1972; Raymond E. Callahan, *Education and the Cult of Efficiency: A Study of Social Forces That Have Shaped the Administration of the Public Schools,* Chicago: The University of Chicago Press, 1970; Harvard Educational Review, *Challenging the Myths: The Schools, The Blacks, and the Poor.* Cambridge, Massachusetts: Harvard Educational Review, 1979; Clarence J. Karier, Paul Violas and Joel Spring, *Roots of Crisis: American Education in the Twentieth Century,* Chicago: Rand McNally College Publishing Company, 1973; and Joan Morrison and Charlotte Fox Zubusky, *American Mosaic: The Immigrant Experience in the Words of Those Who Lived It,* New York: E.P. Dutton, 1980.) Some immigrants "melted"; others got burned or evaporated; and still others never quite made it to the "pot." The existence, for example, of Unico, B'nai Brith, Aspira, NAACP, and innumerable other ethnic organizations proves how little melting was done and how ethnic pride actually has been nurtured as people realize that to be American means to be any one of a number of races, religions, or no religion at all, if one so chooses.

Setting Up the ESL Classroom

Does the physical environment of the ESL classroom have any effect on the quality of learning and on how the individuals who share that learning space feel about each other and themselves? Our professional experience and a longitudinal study show that proper classroom arrangements do have a highly significant though often subtle effect on the teacher and the learner. (Ruth Anne Tschudin, *Educator's Deskbook of Ideas and Activities from Award-Winning Teachers,* West Nyack, New York: Parker Publishing Company, Inc., 1980, 36-49.) To liven up your classroom, why not try one of the following plans:

Plan A: Movable Furniture Setup

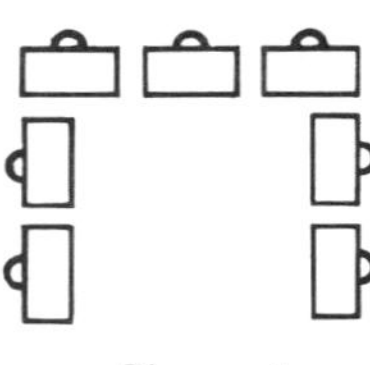

Figure 1

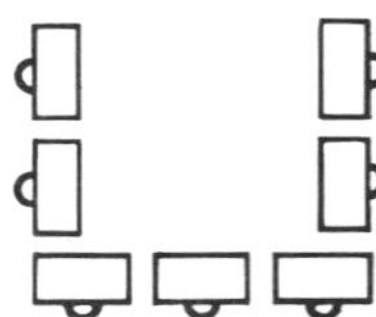

Figure 2

Rule 1 in any class, but in an ESL class in particular, should be: no one should have to face the back of someone else's head. Wherever possible, an arrangement such as those shown in Figures 1, 2, and 3 should be used to facilitate everyone's getting to know each other more quickly. Furthermore, all of these seating styles lend themselves to more natural conversation. Another arrangement that might work well for you is the scattered satellite setup shown in Figures 4 and 5. This arrangement is particularly useful for group work and "round robins." Think back to all those years when your teacher was the only one whose entire face you saw all day during class. How many cowlicks and curls, beehives and D.A.'s were you acquainted with? How many different hip sizes hugged or spilled over from the chair in front of you? Think of all the "cheeks" you were confronted with that were neither rosy nor dancing.

It should be obvious from the four seating arrangements that the actual placement of the teacher's desk is relatively unimportant. No good ESL teacher would be caught sitting at his or her desk during an active ESL lesson or an assessment situation.

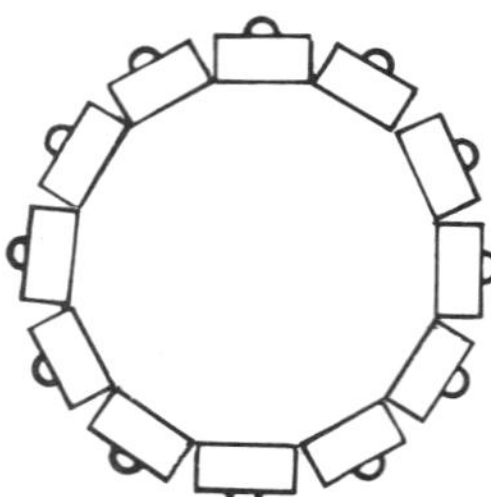

Figure 3

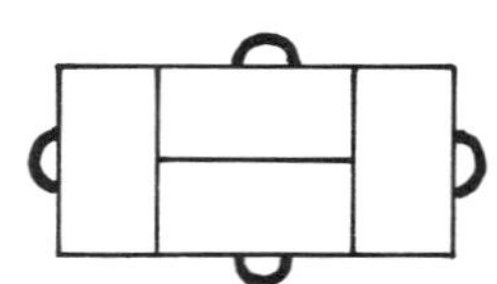

Figure 4

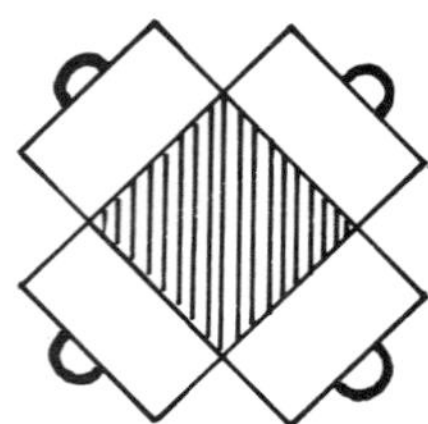

Figure 5

Plan B: Stationary Furniture Setup

If the furniture is fixed to the floor, you can share a groan about it with your students and make the most of a situation that can't be changed. One practical and simple suggestion would be to divide the room into learning and/or activity zones, *e.g.*, where the students can move around, since the furniture can't. (See illustration.)

In any case, have your students shake hands with the people next to, in front of, and behind them at the beginning of each class until they know each other. Using the flexible zone approach, students can/will have different people to greet during the course of the year. The point will probably come where you may wish they weren't so social, but it really helps for them to feel comfortable with their peers and, of course, with you in the language learning situation. Let's face it, learning a new language and culture is a very demanding task. Proper classroom arrangements or rearrangements go a long way toward motivating students to do and act their best, which is, of course, what we all want.

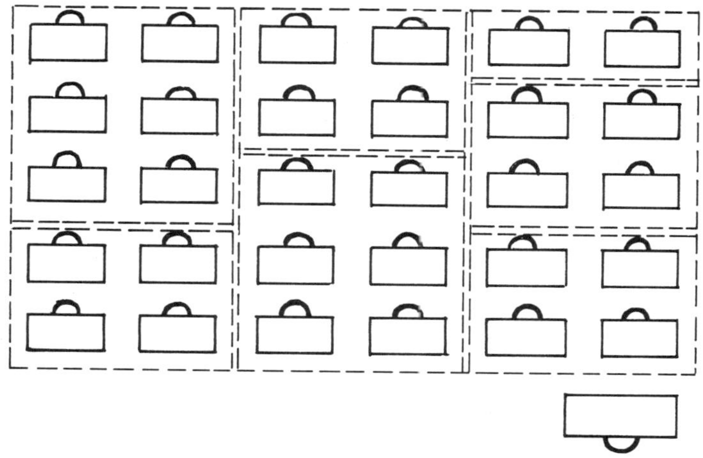

Plan C: Representational System Setup

As you come to know your students better, you can readily spark their desire to master new material and to learn more about themselves and others by grouping learners according to their dominant representational system for learning, *viz.*, visual, auditory, or kinesthetic (feelings, emotions). This type of grouping enables students to:

1. identify a specific learning style strategy that "works" for a topic and leads to further successful experiences.

2. recognize the models who represent the best visual, auditory, and kinesthetic learners in each group and to use these people as resources or "consultants."

3. develop and improve alternative learning strategies when they seem stuck in a learning loop.

4. explore a variety of novel, creative, fun strategies for improving visual, auditory, and kinesthetic memory processes.

Working cooperatively, students and the teacher/facilitator discover each learner's specific learning strategy for completing an assigned task. That learning strategy may be the same or different for each task. Some students are more successful with their strategies than others who have the same dominant representational system. The latter need to find out what is missing or needs changing or updating for their learning strategies to bring them successful experiences. The ultimate goal of this type of grouping is to have a sharing of successful strategies by all groups. In this way, each learner's ability to generate creative solutions/resolutions is greatly expanded. This immediately lightens the burden of the teacher as students accept more and more responsibility for their own learning, regardless of their age.

The authors wish to thank reviewer Marilyn Snider for her suggestion to include Plan C and for the opportunity to review her original professional materials on this topic.

Creative Bulletin Board Ideas

If there is a bulletin board in your room, or any kind of wall space, a fun thing to do is to hang up a map of the world, cut strips of colored paper, give each student a strip and a thumbtack or a gummed star, which they place on their homelands. Then, pinpoint where they are now. Give them each a string to "measure" the distance between the two countries. Later, this map can be a focal point for much conversation about geography, culture, climate, travel, current events, sports, and so forth.

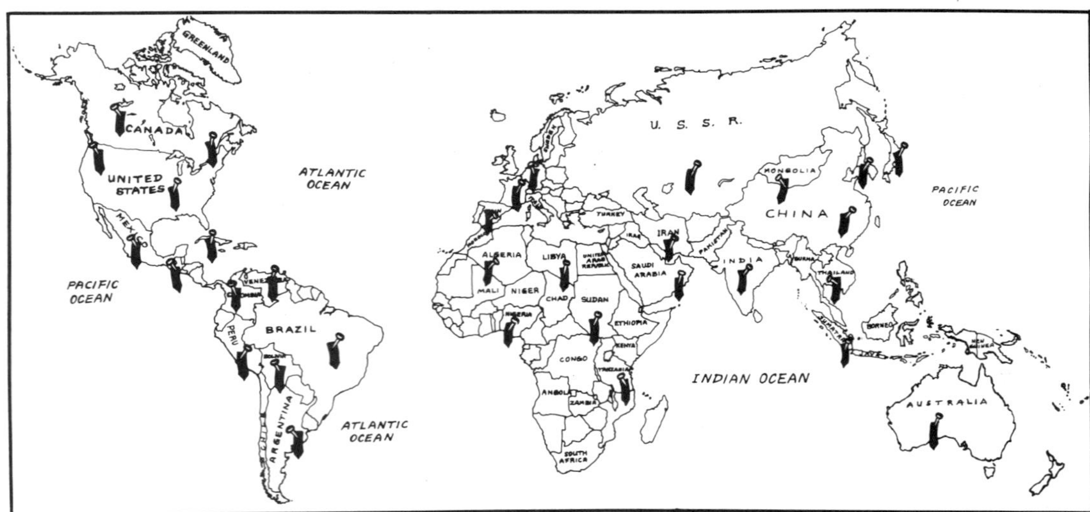

Another bulletin board must: post relevant information, such as ethnic events in the school and/or community, television programs and/or movies of special interest, and/or anything pertinent to their school lives. Anything posted should be discussed to be sure everyone understands. If you don't have sufficient bulletin board space, try this suggestion; it worked beautifully for us. We were offered an opportunity to have our walls painted because they were peeling so badly from years of pictures being taped to them. Instead, we suggested it would be cheaper for the school, and a tremendous boon for the students to have wall-to-wall bulletin boards instead of paint. The custodians cut and hung the boards around the room, and each year the incoming students decorate "their" walls with such things as replicas of great masters, original poems, holiday themes, formal and action photographs of the ESL student body and their families and friends, graduation pictures, and lively multilingual posters with messages such as "Knowledge Is Power" in English as well as in the language of each ESL student.

By gluing a number of 12″ x 12″ cork tiles in the shape of a square or rectangle on a board or directly on the wall, if that's permissible, you can create your own "window on the world." Just nail a pair of shutters or hang a pair of bright curtains on either side of your new cork bulletin board. Let your "window" serve as a backdrop for ever-changing displays of international news items and pictures, as well as student commentaries on current world events. This activity can easily lead to a discussion of journalistic bias, *i.e.,* how different countries cover the same news story, among other things.

Other Suggestions

A bookcase is easily gotten, as is a magazine rack, if you have the space for it. For some students, the magazines you and your friends and relations donate may be the first (or only) English literature to enter their homes. Bring in appropriate magazines, journals, yearbooks, catalogues, and so forth when you're finished with them, especially those with lots of pictures. Tell the class(es) that they are free to take these materials home for their families to enjoy, too. The school and/or local librarian, reading teachers, and other English teachers may also have extra suitable materials that they are willing to share. Check with other organizations and institutions in your community. *Don't be shy.* Ask. All anyone can say is *No.* Don't neglect to ask the custodians. There may be discarded bookcases, magazine racks, or pieces of furniture that can be converted for such use lying idly in closets or woodshops, or simply unused in some less imaginative teacher's room. This activity provides an excellent opportunity to set up an ESL lending library. There is no better way for students to learn organizational skills or to understand how an American library really works than for them to operate their own. Managing their own mini-library will enable them to be knowledgeable users of the school and community library facilities.

Regardless of which seating plan you use, you can also set up a learning "center." Your center can be a table, a specially designated zone or satellite, or even a wall or bulletin board. In short, the learning/activity center can be any place where individuals or groups can do such things as supplemental work, play games, paint, view slides, and so forth. (In one elementary school in Newark, New Jersey, an old gym has been converted into a series of small classes and learning centers. This once infrequently used part of the school is now a bright and enticing hub of excitement and learning.) You may even want to color code the learning center(s) and the materials that belong to each other.

When preparing displays for your class or helping them prepare one of their own, be sure that all displays have a special appeal for and to the learners. One way of ensuring this is to include students in the planning and preparation of displays. Always be sure to hang their work; you may also want to show their progress, *e.g.*, in reading or grammar mastery, by means of a pictorial student skill chart.

If possible, consider having a class pet or pets because of their educational and personal value to your students. This, of course, is especially important for inner city students who may have limited exposure to pets. Plants are also a nice addition to any room. Let the students help care for the pets and plants. They will enjoy it as well as learn from the experience.

The stage is now set for a nonthreatening and enjoyable teaching and learning experience. Your students will probably feel comfortable enough to offer some decorating suggestions or room arrangements of their own. Why not? All that creative energy can be just the spark that's needed to ignite their curiosity and their desire to learn and to please you because you have so obviously gone out of your way to reach them.

The Language Bank

Where potential withdrawals can be saved

It's the first day of school! The *beginner's* ESL class roster lists four Vietnamese, nine Hispanics, two Russians, and one Greek. You speak some Spanish, the Vietnamese pool their limited knowledge of English, the Russians understand a few words, but the Greek boy finds it's not all Greek to him. The gym teacher tells him to have his uniform for tomorrow; the history teacher gives a library assignment, and the youngster ends the day in a vice-principal's office because he went to the bathroom without a pass. As far as the boy can see (and seeing expressions and body language is his *only* way to understand what is being said to him), there is something wrong with going to the bathroom in America. The youngster's ESL teacher is summoned. "Spiro was given the rules and regulations. Why doesn't he understand them? Why did he go to the bathroom without a pass?" You try to explain that the boy just arrived and the rules are not understandable. (See Appendix B, "Sample Welcome Booklet," to avoid this type of unfortunate situation in the future.) Then you find someone who speaks Greek to explain the rules and regulations while Spiro is in the process of learning English.

To do so, you turn to the Language Bank for the name of a colleague or community person who is willing and able to help Spiro survive during those first few overwhelming weeks which can ultimately make the difference in the student's life. Your interest will pay big dividends when Spiro doesn't withdraw.

What Is a Language Bank?

Quite simply, a language bank is a systematic inventory of all the second language resources in one's school, district, and community. Be sure to check with your local senior citizens and handicapped persons' groups. They're terrific, but often untapped, community resources. Everyone will benefit from the interaction.

How to Set Up Your Language Bank

1. Contact the appropriate administrator(s) and the superintendent of schools about establishing a district-wide language bank.

2. After you have secured permission from the administration to proceed with the project, design a 4″ by 6″ index card specifying all the desired information required.

3. Bring the mock-up of the Language Bank Data Card (LBDC) to the above administrators for possible input and official approval.

SAMPLE LANGUAGE BANK DATA CARD
SCHOOL DISTRICT

_____________________, LB Facilitator

Last Name, First	Principal
School	School Telephone No.
Grade(s)	Subject(s)

List languages other than English that you speak fluently:

____

____

____

List languages other than English that you write and read well:

____

____

____

Time when available to help students: ______________________________

---

4. Secure the necessary permission to have the LBDC cards typed and printed "in house," providing, of course, that your district has business education and printing programs in its high school(s). (This is not only economical, but a practical learning and sharing experience.) With today's technology, the quickest, easiest way would be via computer printout.

5. If there are no computer facilities, print up a sufficient number of LBDC's and cover letters. (See Step 6.) LBDC's should be on file in the main office, nurse's office, guidance department, and ESL division in each school. In large districts, a complete set should also be available in the Superintendent's office.

6. Present a draft for an appropriate cover letter to the Superintendent for input and approval. The letter should go out over the Superintendent's signature and should include the value of the Language Bank to the district, an explanation of how the system works, and the date by which cards should be returned to the main office.

SAMPLE COVER LETTER

date

Dear ____________,

Because of the influx of nonnative English speakers in our community, we have started a district-wide LANGUAGE BANK to help these newcomers in situations such as school registration, emergencies, and acculturation. We hope that if you speak, read, write, and/or understand a language other than English, you will become an integral part of our new district's name LANGUAGE BANK by simply filling out the enclosed LBDC cards. Please be sure to complete a separate card for each language you can help with, and return your card(s) by date to person in charge. If you have any questions, please call my office.

Banking on you,

Name of Superintendent

---

7. When Step 6 has been completed, alphabetize the LBDC sets within language groups and see that they reach the designated offices/departments. As you can see, computer printouts are the way to go.

8. Be sure to keep all LBDC files updated during the year and from year to year. This is an important task for the LB facilitator, *i.e.*, the person who is in charge of the project. It's an easy task on the computer.

9. Consider making a separate LBDC file for those people in the community who would be willing and able to assist your students/program. The members of your Parent Advisory Council and your guest speakers would make a good beginning for such a file. Again, you'll need an appropriate cover letter and a sufficient number of printed cards.

Note: Remember, *everyone* is a resource: custodians, cafeteria personnel, secretaries, other students are all valuable sources.

SAMPLE LANGUAGE BANK DATA CARD
COMMUNITY

________________________, LB Facilitator

________________________ ________________________
Last Name, First Home Telephone No.

____
Address

____
(City, State)

List languages spoken fluently other than English:

________________________ ________________________

________________________ ________________________

List languages other than English that you write and read well:

________________________ ________________________

________________________ ________________________

Hours/days when available to help students: ________________________

____

____

The Language Bank can easily be adapted for use in an adult education learning center. These students and the center's personnel should also be sure to complete the *Language Bank Data Card: Community* so that their names could be included in the pool of resources collected by the school district's Language Bank facilitator. We are all in this together.

The School, the Home, the Community

Partners in education

A really good ESL program works effectively when there is understanding and cooperation toward achievement of mutual goals by those most directly involved—students, teachers, and parents—and those indirectly, but often as importantly, involved, the overall community.

While goals might be mutual, value systems may be in conflict, and ESL teachers often find themselves diplomatically suggesting, then urging, and finally insisting, for example, that attendance and punctuality are as much a part of the "American way of life" as hamburgers, pizza, and designer jeans.

Teachers, guidance personnel and administrators also have a great deal of *learning* to do, not only about different concepts of time, but also about the lifestyles and roles of men and women and boys and girls in the native language societies, and how to deal tactfully and properly with them, especially those in most direct conflict with the mores and laws of an America whose current drive appears headed toward a more nonsexist, affirmative action society.

Depending on their geographic origin and socioeconomic status, parents also exhibit different attitudes toward institutions affecting their lives. Educators who are accustomed to parental participation in educational decisions (participation sometimes bordering on interference in the minds of some administrators) often misinterpret lack of active participation of ESL students' parents as a lack of concern for their children's education. For the most part, nothing could be further from the truth. Parents from other countries are more than likely accustomed to leaving the education of their children to the educational institution, revering those involved as having more expertise and wisdom in their professions than they, the parents, could ever have, and respecting that knowledge and ability to educate and discipline their children in the best possible manner. To participate in any way except by a show of gratitude might well be construed by them as interfering and/or insulting, and in many countries, as politically unwise. Coming to America and being confronted almost immediately with requests for active participation in their children's education might be in direct conflict with previous experience. The confusion is often compounded by lack of English language facility and corresponding feelings of embarrassment and inferiority. By sending home bilingual messages, utilizing the parents' native language, and understanding the respective cultures, teachers and administrators can ease the transition from one culture to another. Bilingual parent-teacher, parents-teacher(s), parents-teachers-students conferences (PTS), meetings, and social gatherings can also help.

Parents should know *who* is teaching their children and that *they* can help in the adjustment process. Often, discussion of the move with the student is helpful, as is talking about irreversible situations, e.g., death of a loved one, or those situations which are at least temporarily irreversible, such as political or religious upheavals in their native countries or economic catastrophes which have forced their families to flee. Creating a positive emotional atmosphere for their youngsters enriches and strengthens the parents' role. Learning what is expected by school and community and helping young people to work within that framework can also strengthen their position.

Becoming an active part of their children's education, parents encourage their youngsters to gain the most benefits out of our educational opportunities. Parents can work with the school toward the achievement of mutual goals by getting to know teachers, administrators, and others directly involved in shaping their children's futures. It sounds easy and logical, so why isn't it happening all over the country? Some obvious problems are: language barriers, working parents, preschool children at home making it difficult for parents to attend meetings, past passive roles, cultural and/or socioeconomic barriers leading to preconceived notions about their parents' roles in schools, and problems superseding concern with education.

The ESL Teacher—Resourcefulness Is Our Middle Name

Here are some practical solutions for getting parents and teachers together:

Plan A

For *afternoon or early evening meetings at the school,* free babysitting service can be arranged in a variety of ways:

a. involved parents can take turns with the babysitting chores in a nearby room for a small fee, or

b. paraprofessionals or other capable community people in need of part-time work can be hired to care for the children in a nearby room.

In either case, money can be provided under Chapter 1 funds allocated for just such types of programs. If there is no Chapter 1 program, there are often school or other community funds available for these relatively minor expenditures. Where there are federal- or state-funded projects, there is usually a community component. We have often simply dug into our own pockets and those of others willing and able to "contribute to the cause." If there is no money available, there are usually volunteers. For example, utilize high school or local community college students who might see this as an opportunity for cultural enrichment and/or credit toward a work-study or community service program. This can be worked out beforehand with their teachers and/or administrators. The amount of cooperation when you least expect it can be absolutely astounding! In cases where you teach on an upper-grade level, you can make this a part of your curriculum. Have you ever seen a class where no one volunteered when extra credit was offered and no research, writing, or test-taking was involved? And there is a natural resource in our ESL students, most of whom have had practical experience in the care and handling of younger brothers and sisters. It is also important to form some kind of volunteer babysitting network among parents who are able to participate so that they might be able to help each other under various circumstances during the day and avoid having to keep older children out of school for this purpose. This network could also allow parents to enroll in adult education or college courses. Be sure your meetings are as multilingual as they need be. Send out invitations from the students in their native language and in English enough ahead of time for parents to be able to plan to attend. Request a response so that you are prepared for adequate seating, translators, and refreshments. (Providing refreshments is optional, but a terrific icebreaker if you can swing it. Again, this often depends on Chapter 1 or other funds or your own pockets.)

Arrange the kind of seating and program you want, ahead of time. At the first meeting, you want it social enough to break down some of the interfering barriers but purposeful enough for the parents to see meaning and to want to participate actively in future sessions.

Suggest some topics you would like to discuss and have them talk about what they would like on the next agenda. It's a good idea to form a PTS committee for future program planning and notification of meetings.

At the first meeting, names, addresses, and phone numbers of participants should be gathered for alphabetizing and duplicating so that future program and/or planning committees have access to this information. Constant updating of the list will then fall to the appropriate committee. The more parents you get actively involved, the more opportunity there is for the prestige which comes from being needed.

You don't need us to tell you what topics to discuss or how to go from here—your own special situations will dictate your goal plans. One very important point: it would be a good idea to invite not only all ESL and Bilingual Education teachers, but also any of the faculty, administration, and support services staff (child study team, school nurse, and so forth) who would benefit from and be a benefit to these meetings.

Plan B

Set up coffee klatches. For a complete change of pace, have small-group meetings at the homes of some of the parents. Call a few parents and ask them if they would be willing to use their home as a meeting place to discuss mutual concerns and possible future activities with other parents and teachers and to make phone calls to a few other parents (you supply the phone numbers) and invite them to participate.

Invite one or two ESL teachers and/or support service personnel, administrators, and other interested staff members. You supply the coffee and . . . (including paper plates and cups); parents supply meeting spaces and participants. Procedures are similar to Plan A, only on a smaller, more intimate scale. You are on the parents' turf, making the situation less intimidating for them while providing them with an opportunity to be gracious and hospitable and to participate actively. Depending on the ethnic background(s) involved, there will be variations and adaptations of both plans. These are just suggestion points from which to begin.

Plan C

Pre-arranged visits by the teacher to the home. There are many pros and cons, but we feel most of the cons can be eliminated if visits can be arranged for right after school (or during a weekend or holiday, if no other time is available that is mutually convenient) but long before dinner hours, and if the teacher has become familiar with the culture of the student being visited. If the latter hasn't been done, clearly the ESL teacher needs to complete her or his own education. This should be a number one priority. Plan C is especially important in cases where parents simply cannot come to school because of other problems or commitments.

Plan D

Toward the end of the semester, have a *multicultural, multiethnic festival,* complete with food and entertainment. By now, everyone should know each other to some degree, and different ethnic groups can get together to prepare one or more typical dishes. Students can work on the invitations once the teacher (or teacher and program committee) has arranged for a place (*i.e.,* the school cafeteria) and a date and time have been agreed on. Each ethnic group may surprise you with the amount of talent it can provide: dancers, singers, artists, musicians, poets, photographers, superb chefs and bakers, and so forth. The shrewd ESL teacher will do a little pre-party "educating" of the ESL students concerning acceptable behavior "American style" during entertainment, such as clapping at the end of a performance, giving the performer attention during the performance, and so forth. Some helpful clues about musical tastes, folk dances, eating habits, and the like will also ensure greater understanding of and respect for what might otherwise seem strange, discordant, suggestive, or even downright rude or boring. The teacher should be sure to talk about clean-up committees and any other "delicate" areas so that the cultural event reflects positively on the people who are staging it. For whatever reason, too many others are waiting out there to find fault. We can prevent their being successful with tactful preparations beforehand. It can be very worthwhile (and politic) to invite non-ESL teachers, administrators and, for example, social studies or history classes of native-born Americans to participate in the festivities.

Clearly, ESL instruction to parents is a vital part of a successful educational equilateral triangle. It can be a part of each of the aforementioned plans and can be a subtle part of everyday living by showing parents how to help their children through asking the youngsters to share with their parents what they have learned in English class each day. In addition, most communities offer adult education classes in ESL. If yours doesn't, help get classes started as soon as possible.

Whether through Plan A, or Plan B, or any plan you create, it is extremely important to inform parents and students about various community agencies and organizations that are there to help. Examples might include: Visiting Nurse Service; bilingual agencies (Aspira, CASA, PACO, and so forth); consumer protection services; welfare services; Board of Health; Legal Aid Society; Small Claims Court; local housing authority; civil rights agencies and services; Alcoholism Council and Drug Abuse Board. Many of these are discussed in more detail under those sections dealing with careers and consumer education.

These suggestions work to encourage parents to be a part of their children's education and to participate actively in easing the adjustment problems for their children, to help them understand what is expected by the school and community and how to help the child work within that framework, to encourage a sense of pride and self-worth, to help children to reap the most benefits out of educational opportunities. Parental attendance at those community related sessions of particular interest to them will be very motivating to and supportive of the children and their respective teachers. When the parents are your adult education students, you have an extra opportunity to ease their adjustment in what may be a new dimension in their role as parent. (For further assistance and practical suggestions, see Bertha E. Segal-Swan, *Practical Guide for the Bilingual Classroom (Spanish/English),* San Francisco, California: Alemany Press, 1981.)

Inviting Guests to Your Classroom

A simple how-to

Don't wait until you have exhausted your supply of academic resources for ideas. Get in touch with your human resources. The community you live in is full of professional and nonprofessional people who are willing to come to your classroom to speak to your students. A guest speaker is not only a refreshing change in the routine of the class, but he or she will also provide the L2 learner with an English model or possibly a perspective that is different from yours. Students can become so accustomed to their teacher's voice, accent, and intonation that they can understand only that teacher.

You can either plan a speaker for a particular unit you will be covering or plan a unit around an available guest. You might find the following list helpful in determining the kind of speaker suitable for your teaching unit. People in these jobs are listed in the telephone book.

Topic	Occupation
COMMUNITY SERVICE	ambulance squad volunteer librarian local politician police and firefighter postal worker
FAMILY	family and marriage counselor family planning representative housewife/househusband insurance agent nutritionist psychiatrist psychologist
HEALTH	dietician drug/alcohol counselor nurse, nurse's aide physician

Topic	Occupation
LABOR	bricklayer caretaker construction worker custodian electrician housekeeper mechanic painter
RECREATION	athlete (teenager) backpacking and mountaineering specialist camp counselor disc jockey forest ranger
SCIENCE	environmental/ecological engineer florist laboratory assistant zookeeper
OTHER CAREERS	baker banker bartender computer programmer cosmetician dancer, actor, drama student hotel/motel employee model musician photographer secretary

Organizing the Event

The Guest Speaker Questionnaire (see pages 26–27) helps the speaker know what the presentation should cover and ensures a smooth and efficient use of time. When a volunteer responds, show the questionnaire to your administrators again so they will have a complete understanding of the purpose and the date of the event.

Below are listed several courtesies that will make such an event a pleasant experience for everyone involved:

1. Use official school stationery for your invitation letter and be sure to enclose a stamped, self-addressed envelope with each questionnaire.

2. Use any appropriate films, slides, and records to set the mood of the presentation sometime prior to the actual speech.

3. Invite other classes to the lecture if you feel they might benefit by it. (Be sure to select students and teachers who will not only enjoy the program, but who are also nonthreatening to your class.)

4. Invite administrators and board members to join you on that day.

5. Serve refreshments after the discussion time, if it is permissible in your school.

6. In your introductory comments, be sure to be accurate and brief.

7. Thank your speaker, guests, and class.

8. When it is over, write an article about the event and submit it to the school and local newspapers. Be sure to mention as many students' names as possible.

9. Send a thank-you note to the volunteers. Preferably, have your students write it.

A sample invitation letter is shown on page 25.

SAMPLE INVITATION LETTER:
Resource Persons

Inside Address: ______________________

Date: ______________________

Dear ___(name of guest)___ :

Because of the increase of nonnative English speakers in (name of town/city) , (name of school) offers English as a Second Language (ESL) classes to those students who need to learn the language. Every effort is being made to help these students to learn English as quickly as possible and to become aware of employment possibilities. It would be beneficial for ESL students to meet and speak with successful professional people like yourself.

It is my purpose to invite you to relate your experiences as a (name of occupation) to our ESL students. I would be most appreciative if you could take some time out of your busy schedule to share with us your feelings about the importance of the job you perform. If you have the time to volunteer, please complete and return the enclosed questionnaire in the self-addressed envelope as soon as possible. Your prompt reply will allow me to prepare my classes for your arrival. If you require any additional information or would like to discuss this matter more fully, you may contact me at ___(phone number)___ during school hours.

Sincerely yours,

(your signature)

Department

SAMPLE GUEST SPEAKER QUESTIONNAIRE
(Modify to suit your needs)

Mr.
Ms. ______________________________________ ______________________
(first name) (last name) (occupation)

______________________________ Telephone bus. (____) ______________
(address) home (____) ______________

1. Please indicate if you are available to be a volunteer guest speaker during the month of ____________ when we are doing our unit on careers. If so, which day(s) would be best for you?

2. How much time can you spend at the school?

_____ one classroom period of _____ minutes

_____ two classroom periods of _____ minutes

3. Please check one or more of the following topics that you can/will speak to the students about.

TOPIC A ____

TOPIC B ____

TOPIC C ____

4. Do you need special facilities, props, or audiovisual equipment for your presentation?

____

____

5. How would you like the classroom arranged?
Audience seated in _____ rows _____ circle _____ doesn't matter

_____ other (Please specify.) ______________________________

6. From the topics that are listed in item three, are there any words you will use that need to be defined and discussed with the students *prior* to your arrival? Please list those words you feel the students must know to benefit fully from your presentation.

_______________ _______________

_______________ _______________

_______________ _______________

_______________ _______________

7. Would you like to include a 10-minute question/answer period with the students at the close of your lecture?

_______ yes _______ no

8. Where and when may I contact you to confirm the date and time of your presentation?

____

FOR SCHOOL USE ONLY

DATE _______________

TIME _______________

CLASS PREPARATION _______________

TEACHER _______________

ESL CLASS _______________

Empathy, Sensitivity, Learning

WHO we are teaching comes first

As classroom teachers of ESL, we are faced with students who are here for a variety of reasons, each and all of which can have a profound effect on their ability to learn the target language, *i.e.,* English. People don't leave their families or their native countries behind if all is well. (Many ESL learners who left their countries as adults often live alone or with other co-nationals; for them, feelings of intense isolation and depression are very real and cannot be ignored.) The ESL teacher should be sensitive immediately to his or her students' circumstance. It is a decided advantage to know which students:

a. have had little to say about their move here;

b. have left their parents or families behind to take up residence here with other relatives or friends;

c. have moved from rural to urban environments or vice versa;

d. depending on their point of origin may, for the first time, have encountered variations in color, religion, socioeconomic circumstances, and their own and others' reactions to them;

e. have arrived here as a result of political upheavals in their native land which leave them emotionally homeless and often permanently expatriated;

f. are citizens of the U.S., yet have faced hostility from other citizens.

It is our belief, too, that certain aspects of students' personal lives also affect their willingness and ability to learn, *e.g.,*

a. where they are living and under what conditions;

b. what problems they bring to school each day, including an overriding concern with the political upheavals in their native land;

Planning Successful Field Trips

Probably the single most important ingredient for a successful field trip is the positive attitude of the teacher. If you are confident, your students will behave properly. If you are organized, the trip will run smoothly. And if you are relaxed, the trip will be a delightful experience for all to enjoy.

Field trips are an addition to classroom learning. No matter how short the distance, or how short the time spent away from the classroom, field trips can be highly beneficial. A trip may provide the teacher with the insight into a student's character that will help answer questions about his or her linguistic progress or deficiencies. Taking a field trip is also a good way to check the efficiency of your program. Are your students learning skills they need to survive outside the classroom?

Outlined below are a few helpful guidelines. We urge you to try again, if your field trips have failed in the past. However, if you have never organized a field trip, start planning one today. Here are a few tips to keep in mind:

1. Be calm and confident.

2. With your class, choose an appropriate place to visit.

3. For local field trips, telephone the place you have chosen and ask when they have available time for your group. Have a few tentative dates (pending approval from the administration) in mind when you call. Arrange a date to be confirmed in the near future.

4. Arrange transportation. Check insurance requirements with administration.

5. Submit a field trip request form to the administration. Always state the objective of the trip, listing educational goals. This should encourage the administrator to grant permission. Remember that there are many kinds of trips you can take:

> **a.** *Trips that reinforce a unit of study:* This kind of field trip serves as a beginning or an end for a specific teaching unit. The trip may be in preparation for a test, in which case the trip will serve to strengthen, reinforce, and widen understanding of a particular subject. If the trip is a start of a new unit, it creates enthusiasm and arouses attention.
>
> **b.** *Trips in which students perform a particular activity:* An example would be any outing where students are asked to complete a simple task; for instance, jotting down all the things that are going on in an airport terminal or correctly identifying animals at a zoo. This kind of trip affords spontaneous learning, realistic circumstances, and heightened awareness.

c. *Recreational trips:* For some reason, these are the hardest to justify. Inform your administration that many sports are new to your students. They know little about American sports and have had little, if any, introduction to them. This is the time you plead not only for a bilingual curriculum but for a bicultural one, as well.

d. *Trips of cultural value:* Theater productions, concerts, and festivals fall under this heading. In your request, emphasize the role of the school in providing these types of experiences to students who might otherwise *not* be exposed to them. These trips can provide an introduction to the American "high cultural" scene and create awareness of another avenue of career exploration. Word your request with phrases such as "supplementing the experiences offered in the home," "stimulating intellectual growth," and "expanding horizons." Make every effort to keep expenses to a minimum. Before presenting a project to the students, research resources for supplemental funding for those students who might not otherwise be able to participate.

6. Don't get discouraged. Arrange and rearrange, if need be, until you have the trip exactly as you want it.

7. Prepare the students:

a. inform them well in advance about what to bring and how to dress;

b. talk about proper bus and public building etiquette;

c. inform them that school rules relating to smoking, drinking, and so forth will be in effect on the school trip;

d. spark their enthusiasm by showing pictures, postcards, and brochures of where you'll be taking them.

8. Collect permission slips and money in advance of the scheduled departure date. (Generally, permission slips are not required for any student over eighteen. Check the insurance/age regulations in your district for specifics.)

9. The day of the trip, STAY CALM. To maintain the sometimes sagging spirits that accompany a long bus ride, sing songs, play games, tell jokes and riddles. If you are at a loss for entertaining your students on the bus, head for your school or public library. They always have a section that includes games and tips for traveling with students of all ages.

Suggested Field Trips

In all probability, there are many interesting, exciting, and educational field trip possibilities available to your students within reasonable distance from your school. Here are some inexpensive field trip ideas:

Industrial Plants and Agricultural Centers
orchards, canneries, mills, beverage manufacturers, clothing manufacturers, wineries, bakeries, food processors, mines, factories, automotive manufacturers, shipbuilders, aircraft manufacturers

Artistic and Historic Sites
historic shrines and monuments, museums, Indian reservations, restorations, architectural walks, concerts, theater productions, festivals, an artist's studio, state capitol buildings

Communication Centers
television and radio stations, newspaper offices, airports, ports, locks, subways, commercial boat trips

Scientific Study Centers
aquariums, zoos, archeology digs, beaches, planetariums, caves, science museums, laboratories, dams, rivers, ponds, wildlife preserves

Environmental Study Centers
ecology walks, recycling plants, local/county environmental education centers

Recreation Areas
Sports stadiums, parks, amusement parks, hiking, skiing, and camping sites, other sports locales

Community Facilities
hospitals, civic buildings (court, jail, library, fire and police departments), county colleges, state colleges and/or universities

Local Cemeteries
to learn the history of a community and its people: the "old" names in the town, how long people lived, what they died from, and so forth.

Activities for the Classroom

Welcome Handbooks

An easy bilingual project

The creation of bilingual welcome handbooks put together by *advanced* ESL classes (See Appendix B) is another exciting adoptable-adaptable plan for your classes' needs and abilities, regardless of their age or grade level.

The original idea for our bilingual handbooks came from a suggestion from the late Ruth Crymes at a secondary school presentation at the Miami TESOL Convention, 1977. She discussed the creation of a handbook to help male Korean students at the University of Hawaii who needed to be briefed on cultural differences between the United States and Korea. She specifically mentioned the custom of males walking arm-in-arm or with an arm around the other's shoulders, in typical Korean fashion. A handbook was developed to point out some typical and atypical customs as viewed by a majority of the dominant culture. She encouraged her audience to beware of those differences which could be a source of embarrassment or misunderstanding to newcomers and to have students who have experienced adjustment to the new culture develop bilingual handbooks for future arrivals.

Around mid-semester, discuss the various problems and feelings that class members encountered when they entered their first American school. For example:

1. Were they eager? apprehensive? just plain scared?

2. What were other people's reactions to them?

3. How long did it take them to feel "part" of the school? What moment or what incident led to their realization that they now "belonged"?

4. What advice would they give to newcomers that might help them adjust more rapidly to their new surroundings?

This Worked for Us—Try It

1. Let students from each language background get together in groups (not to exceed five in a group, if possible). If the majority is from one language background, they can still work with people of their own choosing who are also speakers of the same language. Later, their combined efforts will be one handbook. Each group or team should appoint a scribe to take notes, and a captain to organize the group's efforts.

2. After ten minutes or so of group discussion, each member should write her or his suggestions for new students on how to cope with and adjust to the new school. Whichever language they choose to write in will have to be translated to the second language, too. Language preference is immaterial at this stage. You might suggest they include something about such things as:

a. major school rules and regulations;

b. graduation requirements;

c. guidance and other school-related services;

d. extracurricular activities;

e. observed cultural differences which might affect them.

Other bits of helpful information from what was elicited during their earlier responses to your questions should also be considered.

3. While students are working in their teams, walk around and lend an ear, but no more, unless you are invited to do so. Don't worry if one language team has only one or two people. Tell them they are pioneers in the school, and if you need to explain *pioneers,* great! You've got another lesson to teach, and *you* can learn about the pioneers in their countries.

4. For homework, ask each student to write his or her list of suggestions in English and in the native language so that the team can work on them the next day.

5. In class, let the team members discuss each other's comments, make changes, revisions, and suggestions, and spend as many periods as necessary (no more than three periods of 40 to 60 minutes should be necessary) before presenting the material to you.

6. Go over each language team's work, correcting the English where necessary and enlisting the aid of a teacher, guidance counselor, or other staff member with the same native language as the students, to be sure the Spanish, Gujarati, Polish, Greek, Vietnamese, or whatever is as correct as possible. No such staff skills? Try the local community college. Stop at the local hospital. Generally, where there is a large group who speaks the same language, there's at least one nurse, intern, or interpreter who can and will check the native language portion for you and be delighted to do it. Often, too, there is a member of the local clergy who is familiar with the particular language group you are working with. And don't neglect parents as a human resource. Many may speak "exotic" languages (exotic to us, that is) and may be people of education in their native countries. They would be flattered to have a useful role in their children's education and in improving relations between new arrivals and the dominant culture. *Don't let little things stand in the way of good classroom management and creativity. Be resourceful.* If you're going to feel defeated, let it be from something monumental (for example, planning a bilingual handbook with a class of Hmongs, who have no written language).

7. Once the correctness of the language has been established, let the teams work toward proper sequencing of ideas, proofreading, layout, a title page, and a credits page. (This might be a good time and place to teach a simple lesson about protecting one's work through a copyright.) If there are typists and artists in your class, or those familiar with computers and word-processing, solicit their help in getting the material on ditto sheets or discs for easy reproduction. Try enlisting the aid of the print shop teacher, if one is available. Have his or her class take on the "publishing" of the handbooks as a project, if this is agreeable and is in accordance with school policy. If your school doesn't have such facilities, community colleges or branches of nearby universities or local business and civic groups would probably help. Just ask! Where a media center specialist or audiovisual aids director exists, she or he might offer suggestions for easy, inexpensive duplicating.

The best way to ensure success is to present the project first to your school principal, tell him or her the purpose of the project for future newcomers, and how you plan to execute it. Ask his or her advice on whether the print shop, graphic arts, media specialist, and so forth could be involved. It's amazing what you can accomplish when administrators are asked for advice or suggestions and made to feel the result was *their* idea. All you have to do is present your plan by:

a. showing how these helpful handbooks will prevent many problems familiar to administrators from arising in the future because there will now be a guide given to every non-English speaking newcomer in his or her native language, as well as in English.

b. having your plan completely clear in your mind, including how you will get the collating and stapling done—something you can discuss with whomever is doing the reproducing. If it turns out to be your job, a sure-fire way to get it done quickly is to set the pages in order on desks around the room, have the students form a line and walk around the room picking up a page as they go along until they reach the student(s) with staplers at the end. It's a change of pace and it takes so little time; if you keep it businesslike, you'll be finished in one class session (and depending on the size of the room, maybe a little dizzy). Think of it as jogging, ESL style.

c. being ready to answer those questions you know you can anticipate with regard to money, time, personnel involved, and so forth.

d. showing the value to the school of:

1. team teaching;

2. students being involved in *practical* projects and reinforcing their own learning by helping others;

3. new students being made to feel welcome and knowledgeable about their new surroundings: what they can expect, and what is expected of them.

You, yourself, will experience at least two highs: *one,* when you see the faces of the "authors" as you pass out the finished copies of the handbooks they have created, complete with their names on the list of credits, and *two,* when you see the appreciative faces of your new students as they receive this nonthreatening booklet so different from the myriad of other papers too often heaped on them the first day of school. How comforting to know someone your own age has gone through the process, survived, and cared enough about you to try to ease your burden these first confusing days. And what an immediate link to "new, old friends."

8. When the handbooks are ready to be distributed, students can deliver them to other ESL teachers, bilingual teachers, and any others you or they feel are appropriate. Be sure they deliver copies to the superintendent of schools, Board of Education, principal, vice principal(s), guidance counselor(s), school nurse(s), child study team, and so forth. Each delivery means some kind of communication between ESL students and native English-speaking staff, and this in itself is valuable.

> **a.** Through role playing, you might want to prepare some kind of introduction with the students beforehand so no one feels too shy or uncomfortable.
>
> **b.** You might also want to inform staff of your ESL students' forthcoming visit to avoid unexpected traumas for anyone.

Be sure to let the "authors" keep several copies of the Welcome Booklets for themselves. Many of our students sent copies of the handbooks they had helped to write to grandparents and relatives in their native countries as Christmas gifts or birthday cards. There is no magic like the magic of one's name in print!

Once you've completed the bilingual handbooks, you may want to revise different sets from year to year or, more practically, every few years. Different classes, as well as changes in our own culture, will dictate different ideas and necessary revisions. Your first handbook will be a testament of your own and your class's creativity and school spirit.

If your students are nonreaders and/or nonwriters, the discussion and ideas can come from them, and *you* can write the English portion of what they say. Then, have parents, aides, or whatever resources you can tap do the translating into those languages you don't know. How much more interesting and exciting to learn to read through recognition of one's own thoughts, experiences and words than those of a Dolch or Maxwell! You can make flash cards, charts, and/or booklets giving the "authors'" names. We can almost guarantee an increased reading interest level and effort as Juan or Khaled recognizes his name for the first time and wants to know what golden words he has authored. Remember, for easy evaluation of this unit and those to follow, see Master 12 at the back of the book.

Look Who's Teaching Now

How-to projects

They've got those words bottled up in there. How to get them out in some kind of organized, meaningful fashion? Have your students do a five-minute "How-To" in front of the class. Explain that among the benefits to them will be:

1. organizing their thoughts to make them clear to others;

2. speaking in front of a familiar group is good practice for trying their new language in the outside world;

3. teaching something to someone else:

a. adds to their stature and builds confidence and motivation, and

b. reinforces their own learning.

You might want to demonstrate your own "How-To" with this sample lesson or something of your own.

SAMPLE HOW-TO PROJECT TITLE PAGE

How to Remove Pet Stains From Your Rug

by

Jean Maculaitis-Cooke

and

Mona Scheraga

**** METHODS ****

Notional Functional

Total Physical Response

Sample How-To Project ESL Lesson Plan

I. TITLE OF PROJECT

How to Remove Pet Stains from Your Rug

II. TARGET SECOND LANGUAGE (L2) POPULATION

This lesson has been specifically designed for intermediate multilingual-multiethnic ESL students enrolled in an adult education learning center in an urban community, *i.e.,* Tall Timbers Adult Learning Center, Eugene, Oregon.

III. OBJECTIVES

The aims of this lesson are to teach the above-mentioned L2 learners to:

1. listen carefully and comprehend simple, everyday English;

2. follow simple oral and written L2 directions presented in sequential order;

3. increase their L2 vocabulary, using "real life" words and helpful procedures;

4. use newly acquired L2 vocabulary to demonstrate "how-to" to others;

5. remove a stain from a rug without ruining it;

6. become aware and ever mindful of the safety factors involved in using common household cleansers;

7. administer proper first aid in the event of an accident, *e.g.,* burning of the skin and eye.

IV. TEACHING METHODS

The *notional functional technique* and the *total physical response approach* will be used to teach this lesson, *i.e.,* using language in meaningful "real life" situations.

V. PROCEDURE

First Session

Step 1: Obtain carpet remnants from local department or carpet store, making sure that there is a sufficient number for the class.

Step 2: Cut up carpet remnants so that each student has his or her own.

Step 3: Apply simulated stain approximating pet stain to each small square of carpet needed for this lesson.

Step 4: Obtain and display various types of stain removers and equipment. (See VII, "MATERIALS".)

Step 5: Distribute mimeosheets with vocabulary to be used during demonstration lesson.

Step 6: Hold up and name each item as it appears in the vocabulary list. (See VIII, "VOCABULARY".)

Step 7: Explain problem and have an open discussion to generate interest, *e.g.*,

a. How many of you have a pet?

b. What kind of pet do you have?

c. Is your pet housebroken?

d. If so, who trained your pet?

e. Does your pet ever have "accidents" at home?

f. What do those nasty pet stains do to your rug/carpet?

g. Can they be safely and inexpensively removed without damaging the rug/carpet?

Step 8: Hold up the rug stain; point to the stain. Begin demonstration of method(s), explaining while demonstrating. Be sure each person understands as you show the various techniques, such as: "Rub in a circular motion," "Blot," and so forth. Use a separate square for each cleaning agent. Lay rug squares aside according to directions for use of each agent.

Step 9: Discuss safety factors involved in using each agent.

Step 10: Discuss emergency measures in case of accident.

Step 11: Conduct question and answer/open discussion period.

Next Session

Step 12: Review material covered in first session.

Step 13: Where necessary, complete procedures according to directions for specific cleansers.

Step 14: Review procedures.

Step 15: Distribute written directions and a small square of carpet to each student and assign cleansing agents at random to each student.

Step 16: Have students demonstrate and explain procedure for removing carpet stain with assigned cleansing agent.

Step 17: Use criterion-referenced rating scale to evaluate each student's performance of the task. (See IX, "EVALUATION".)

VI. DURATION

From introduction to conclusion, including student evaluation, this lesson will take approximately 80 minutes.

VII. MATERIALS

The following is a list of materials to be used with this lesson:

1. small square of carpet/rug—already stained
2. can/bottle of club soda or a pail of clear cool water
3. kosher salt
4. spot remover
5. brush or sponge
6. blotter or sponge
7. rug deodorizer
8. first aid kit
9. hankie for crying when stain doesn't come out!

VIII. VOCABULARY

The following is a list of L2 vocabulary words to be used with this lesson:

absorb
accident
back and forth
blot
brush
burn
can
careful
carpet
caution
circular motion
clean, cleaning agent
cleanse
club soda
contents
danger
Don't rub.
external
emergency treatment
fatal
feces
first aid
Follow directions.
harmful ingredients
hints
housebroken
internal
kosher salt
nap
odor
pail
poison
powder
rectangle
results
rub
rug
spot remover
square
stain
swallow
tips
train
urine
vacuum
vomit
wait
Watch out.

IX. EVALUATION

Each student or language learning team is actually required to teach his/her/their lesson to someone *before* demonstrating it to the class. By following this preliminary procedure, each person or team will be able to ensure the success of their project and increase the quality of their teaching.

Each student's classroom performance will be assessed according to the following rating scale:

SAMPLE CRITERION-REFERENCED RATING SCALE

GRADE	PERFORMANCE DESCRIPTION
A	Student able to follow *all* simple oral and written directions.
B	Student able to follow *most* simple oral and written directions.
C	Student only able to follow simple oral and written directions with *some repetition*.
D	Student only able to follow simple oral and written directions with *many repetitions*.
E	Student *totally confused* and unable to follow simple oral and written directions. Further investigation needed to find reason(s) for student's failure to perform task satisfactorily *e.g.*, lack of proper concentration and/or motivation.

X. OVERVIEW

Evaluate (in writing) the degree of success of the entire lesson. Be sure to consider such relevant questions as:

a. Did the lesson work well?

b. If not, why not?

c. If so, why?

d. Would you do it differently next time, that is, if there is a next time?

e. What can be done to improve the lesson? (Get input from class.)

NOTE: OTHER POSSIBILITIES

How to:

- change a flat tire
- apply for a Social Security card
- bake a cake
- make a favorite ethnic dish (Bring in finished product first.)
- play a favorite instrument (Bring in guitar, bongos, flute, etc., for demonstration.)
- weave a basket, and so forth.

Suggested Activities Using Inexpensive or Free Materials

Here are a dozen interesting things to do with your students. These suggested activities could be a starting point for developing your own ideas. (Part of this section originally appeared in *The Creative ESL Secondary School Teacher: A Practical Handbook of Inexpensive Materials and Successful Techniques,* by Beverly Amster and Jean D'Arcy Maculaitis.) You may be surprised at how many good teaching and learning ideas you and your students will come up with from these activities, using simple, easily available materials. *Don't feel limited by the objectives that have been indicated at the beginning of each activity.* The time and effort will still have been well spent even if every objective is not met. These activities are meant to be enjoyable as well as educational.

After your class has participated in an activity, evaluate it in ways that will help you plan the next one, *e.g.,*

- Was everyone able to take part?
- How could I have improved the use or distribution of materials?
- Which portion of this activity proved most useful as a teaching/learning experience? Which was the least useful?
- For which proficiency level was it most appropriate?
- Is this activity worth repeating? Why? Why not?
- What further use can be made of the "finished product" cognitively and affectively?
- Did my students enjoy themselves?

It is important to note that in each case the level of ESL proficiency will dictate just how far you can go with the twelve activities that follow. Each can be adapted for any age group.

ACTIVITY 1:

"Hot and Cold Game" *(beginners)*

OBJECTIVES: *To guess the picture that another student has selected; to learn simple social skills and appropriate interactional behavior; to review material/ vocabulary already presented; to experience success and fun playing a game in the new language; to generate and comprehend natural language at the basic beginner level*

1. Reproduce a workbook page containing twenty or so pictures illustrating some skill or grammatical point that needs to be reviewed, *e.g.*, pictures of objects that begin with the /t/ sound or pictures of various animals, parts of the body, and the like. A page with five rows of four or five pictures is best, although you can vary this to suit your own needs.

2. PLAYER 1 selects a picture but does not tell which one until the other player(s) guess it. ("Hot and cold" is best played with no more than three people in a group.)

3. PLAYER 2 and/or 3 take turns asking PLAYER 1, "Is it the ____________?" (For example, "Is it the brown dog?") The guesser must point to the picture being referred to.

4. PLAYER 1 has to respond for each question with "hot" if the picture guessed borders on the one selected, "warm" if it is close to the one chosen, "cold" if the one guessed is far away, and "cool" if it is somewhat closer than the farthest possible point, which would result in a "cold" response.

5. This interaction continues until either PLAYER 2 or 3 narrows down the possibilities and guesses the selected picture.

6. The player who guesses the correct picture then asks PLAYER 1, "Tell me/ us why you like this picture." Then he or she chooses the next picture to be guessed.

On a more advanced level, this can be played like "Twenty Questions," with students getting to practice formation of *yes/no* questions.

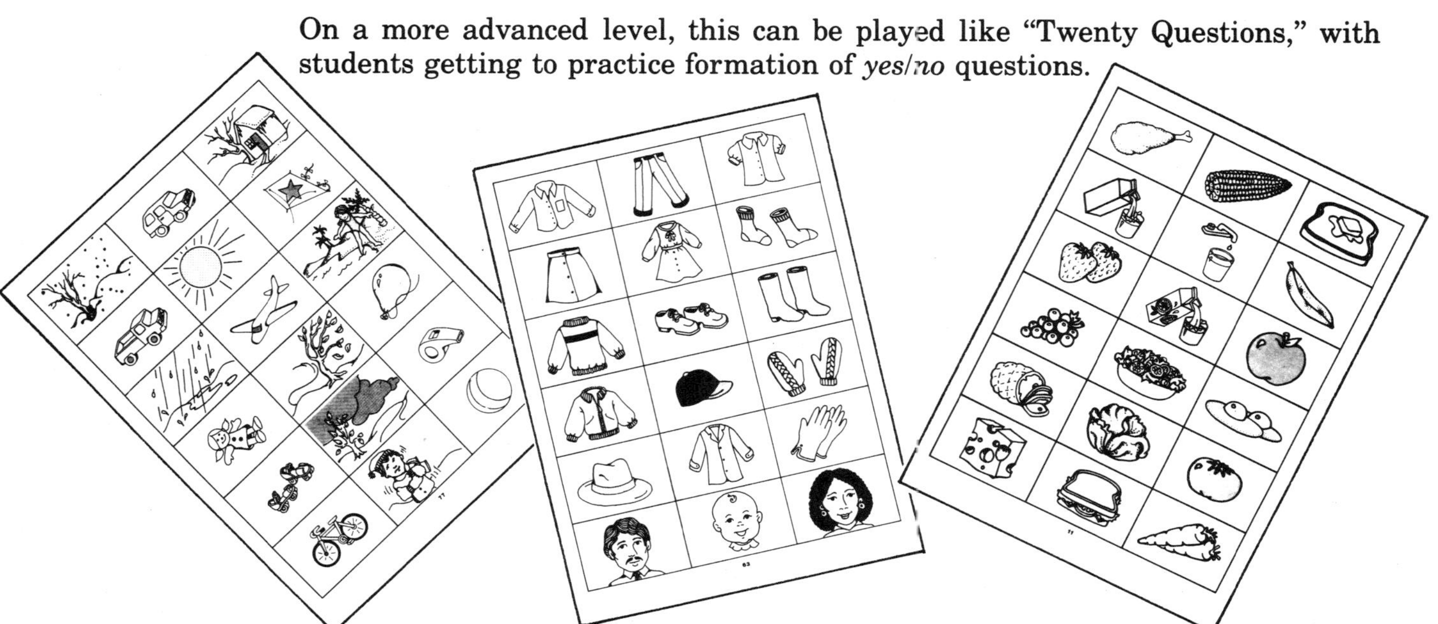

ACTIVITY 2:

Learning with Paint Chips *(beginners)*

OBJECTIVES: *To learn the names of colors; to gain practice with different grammatical forms*

Here's an idea for you! Ask your local hardware store clerk if you can borrow an old set of sample paint chips. You know, those tiny squares of graduated colors you use to select the paint for your home. Well, they can be a great source of ideas for teaching. For example, they can be used to teach:

1. Colors
   e.g., What color is this? Show me the navy blue square.

2. Comparison of adjectives
   e.g., Which blue is calmer/darker/lighter?

3. The conditional tense
   e.g., If you need to paint your kitchen/living room/bedroom, which color would you choose? I would choose ________________.

ACTIVITY 3:

Constructing a Candy House *(beginners through advanced)*

OBJECTIVES: *To build a candy house; to learn about the parts of a house; to learn to work in teams; to learn to follow directions; to increase L2 listening-comprehension skills*

Materials

empty milk carton	confectioners sugar (one box)
a ruler	a bowl
a pen	a spoon
scissors	a knife
tape	3 eggs
graham crackers (one box)	candy

Team Instructions

Part I: Forming the Roof

1. Open up the top of the carton and cut the top off.

2. Wash and dry inside and outside of carton thoroughly.

3. Now, measure 2½″ down from the top at each corner. Cut to the 2½″ mark. (See Figure 1.)

4. Measure the width of one side. Find and mark the middle, 1″ down from the top. This is the front. Do the same on the opposite side. This is the back.

5. Draw a line connecting the 2½″ marks to the middle, forming the sides of the roof. (See Figure 2.)

6. Cut along the lines you have just made.

7. Fold in the sides and tape them to the front and back. (See Figure 3.)

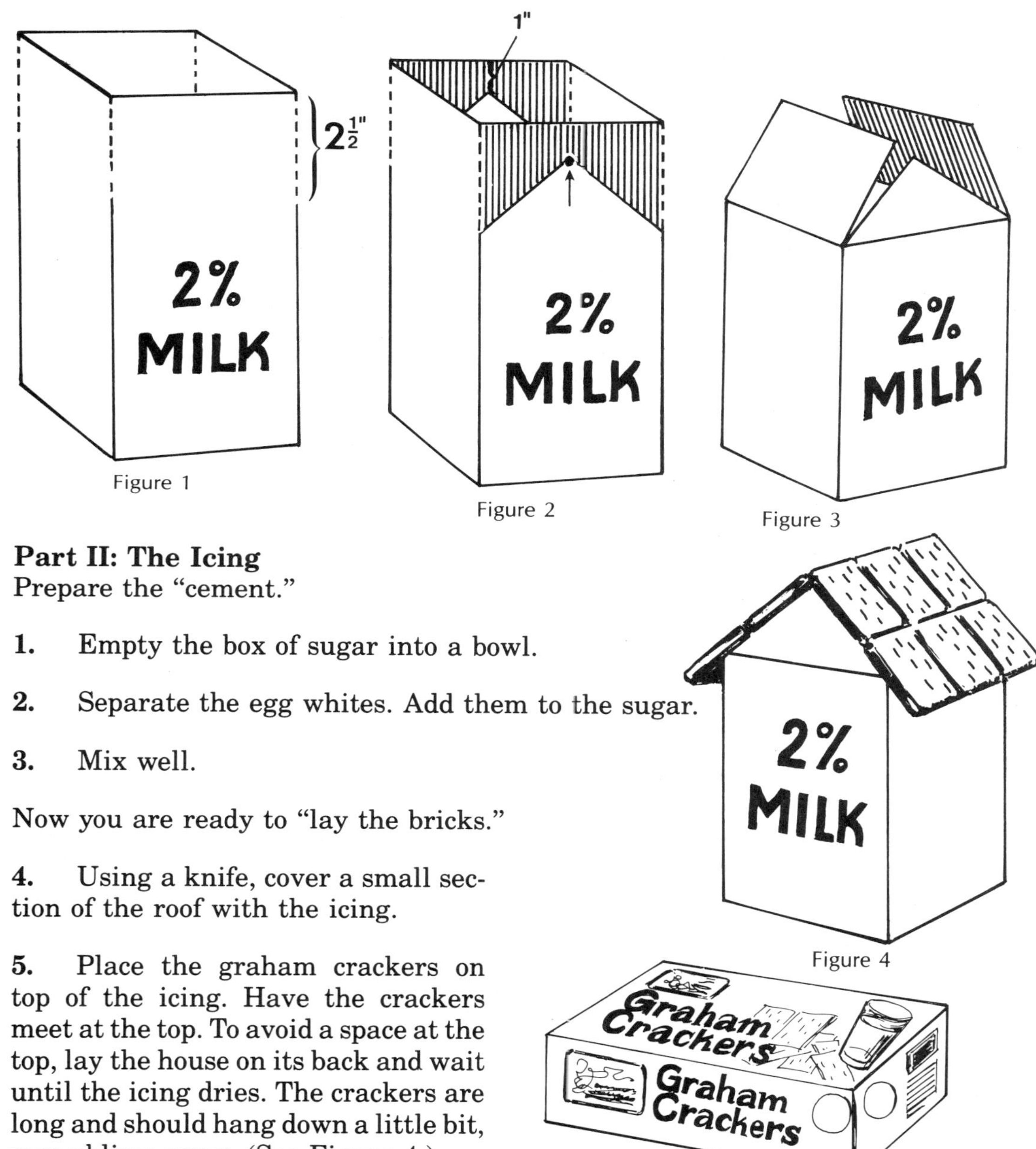

Figure 1

Figure 2

Figure 3

Figure 4

Part II: The Icing
Prepare the "cement."

1. Empty the box of sugar into a bowl.

2. Separate the egg whites. Add them to the sugar.

3. Mix well.

Now you are ready to "lay the bricks."

4. Using a knife, cover a small section of the roof with the icing.

5. Place the graham crackers on top of the icing. Have the crackers meet at the top. To avoid a space at the top, lay the house on its back and wait until the icing dries. The crackers are long and should hang down a little bit, resembling eaves. (See Figure 4.)

6. Working one side at a time, continue the process by covering the box with icing and "gluing" on the crackers.

7. Using a knife, cut the crackers to fit the irregularly shaped spaces. (Remember that it is always easier to ice the box rather than the cracker.)

Part III: Decoration
The work is over and the fun begins!
Here are some ideas for decorating your house after it has completely dried.

a. Let your imagination run wild to create windows, doors and a chimney.

b. Green lifesavers can be a door wreath.

c. Drip icing on the roof for a "snowy" effect.

d. Put an edible chocolate Santa in the chimney.

e. Use gum drops around the edges for Christmas lights.

f. Small cheese crackers make great shingles.

Part IV: Presentation
When the holiday house has been completed, place it in a low cardboard box, big enough for the following additions: set it down on a ground of "snow drifts," using cotton (or the less practical but very attractive ground of shredded coconut). Depending on how "into" the project you and your class are and what your time and financial constraints are, you can embellish your house with a sesame seed or peanut "stone" walkway, a flagstone path of heartshaped cookies, and evergreen trees made of toothpicks that have been broken in half and attached to spearmint leaves, (approximately three $10\frac{3}{4}$-ounce bags of spearmint gumdrops) leaf tip down. Use $6'' \times 2\frac{3}{4}''$ styrofoam cones around the base of the house and put the "trees" into the cones. Three cones are needed in all, one for each bag of spearmint leaves. With toothpicks, attach miniature gumdrops to each tree. Place miniature plastic or wooden animals and people outside your house to complete the winter holiday scene. It would be wise to cover the entire project with some form of plastic or Saran-type wrap. If you're working with adults, let them write the "recipe" for the project so they can try it at home, too.

ACTIVITY 4:

Studying Maps *(beginner through advanced)*

OBJECTIVES: *To learn how to read maps; to learn the vocabulary used in giving directions and explaining distances; to learn in detail about a particular place of interest*

Necessary vocabulary for giving simple directions in English:

make a turn bear hang a follow to the	} right, left	straight ahead go down make a U turn intersection

Either you or one of your students can draw a simple map on the board. The history or social studies teacher may also be able to provide you with various maps, blank and otherwise. At the elementary level, road sign kits and games are commercially available, or you can easily make your own signs on oaktag. In a beginning class, students can learn to "show and tell" how to get to their house from school. Tell them you're coming for dinner and you need very specific directions. *Where* do you turn? *Where* do they live: upstairs, downstairs, in front, in back, in the middle of the block, on the corner?

If you or one of your colleagues is a member, you may write to the Automobile Association of America for special road maps of the fifty states and Puerto Rico. Advanced students can work individually or in groups to answer questions about the states and their highways, or they can plan a cross-country trip, pooling their efforts to determine the shortest/most scenic trip. However, be sure the students know the meaning of the symbols on the map, which are explained in the key. Ask distance-related and size-proportioned questions such as:

1. Which city is farther north, Los Angeles or San Diego?

2. Which highway would be the fastest and most direct route from New York to California?

3. Name a city to the south which is larger in size than ________________.

This could be a team effort between you and a social studies colleague, as could the following fun projects:

1. Construct a small-scale model of your town or a portion of it.

2. Mark out a course in a nearby park. With the students in teams, have them follow separate maps to find a hidden "treasure"; this "treasure" should have been placed by you in an inconspicuous spot. Add many "turns" to keep the students thinking.

3. Use the school library or media center. Give the class assignments which lead to the use of a globe, atlas, or encyclopedia. Perhaps you can have a more meaningful lesson by relating the map study to a particular area that is especially important in the news that week. Or, base your discussion on one of the maps found in the *National Geographic* magazine.

4. Depending on the size of your *advanced* class, this assignment can be done individually or in groups. Choose a specific area of study; for example, the American West. Request different kinds of maps of the area. When you have collected a few of them, write five to seven questions about each map on an index card. Attach the card to the appropriate maps and give each student or group of students their own map and question card. Circulate around the room and check their answers. As one group finishes, have them exchange cards and maps with another group. Continue until all groups have completed all questions.

ACTIVITY 5:

Playing Presidential Bingo *(intermediate through advanced)*

OBJECTIVES: *To learn the names of the presidents; to learn to play Bingo; to improve L2 listening and reading skills*

Presidential Bingo is identical to regular Bingo except that presidents' names are used instead of numbers. The students will enjoy the game while learning the names of the presidents of the United States.

Playing Bingo is also a fun way to learn the names of the other people in class, streets in town, parts of the body, family names (*e.g.*, aunt, grandfather, etc.), or whatever is relevant to what you're teaching/reviewing at the time. In keeping with the increasing emphasis on ESL in the content areas, Bingo is also an easy introduction to or review of the names of the cities, states, and other pertinent facts that will help speed your students' integration into the mainstream.

1. Ahead of time, prepare lists of the presidents' names and the Bingo charts to distribute to your students. Bingo charts can be made on ditto masters by drawing a box with five horizontal and five vertical squares in it. The middle square is marked "free" and the letters B-I-N-G-O are written on the top line. Allow one letter for each square. Arrange two charts on the ditto sheet.

2. When students have the charts and lists, they must select any president's name and print it in a square. All squares must be filled. No name can be repeated.

3. Give out chips to each player. (Obtain the chips from a regular Bingo game or cut up your own.)

4. Select a caller who checks off the names on the list as he or she selects them randomly.

5. The students cover the space containing the president's name as it is called. The person who covers a full line vertically, horizontally, or diagonally wins. He or she may then be the caller.

6. Have small prizes (pencils, erasers) for winners.

LIST OF PRESIDENTS OF THE UNITED STATES

1. George Washington
2. John Adams
3. Thomas Jefferson
4. James Madison
5. James Monroe
6. John Quincy Adams
7. Andrew Jackson
8. Martin Van Buren
*9. William Henry Harrison
10. John Tyler
11. James Polk
*12. Zachary Taylor
13. Millard Fillmore
14. Franklin Pierce
15. James Buchanan
+16. Abraham Lincoln
17. Andrew Johnson
18. Ulysses S. Grant
19. Rutherford B. Hayes
+20. James A. Garfield
21. Chester A. Arthur
22. Grover Cleveland
23. Benjamin Harrison
24. Grover Cleveland
+25. William McKinley
26. Theodore Roosevelt
27. William H. Taft
28. Woodrow Wilson
*29. Warren G. Harding
30. Calvin Coolidge
31. Herbert Hoover
*32. Franklin D. Roosevelt
33. Harry S. Truman
34. Dwight D. Eisenhower
+35. John F. Kennedy
36. Lyndon B. Johnson
37. Richard M. Nixon
38. Gerald Ford
39. James Carter
40. Ronald Reagan

KEY
*died in office
+ assassinated

ACTIVITY 6:

Using Telephone Books *(beginners through advanced)*

OBJECTIVES: *To learn how to use a telephone book; to learn about synonyms; to learn how to handle everyday situations, using the Yellow Pages*

Telephone books, especially the Yellow Pages, can provide the ESL teacher with countless ideas for lexical and practical skill games to use in the classroom. (See "They've Got Your Number," page 60, on using the telephone as a teaching tool for a complete unit plan. See also Appendix C.)

ACTIVITY 7:

Using Clothing Lists *(intermediate to advanced)*

OBJECTIVES: *To learn how to request service from a dry cleaner; to learn about clothing and its care; to learn the vocabulary of requests; to increase awareness of syntactic differences between L2 questions and statements*

Clothing lists are obtainable from your friendly cleaners. The next time you take in your clothes to be cleaned, ask for a few. If you explain how you propose to use them, we're sure most cleaning establishments will oblige. When you accumulate enough for your class, you can try these activities:

1. Write a dialogue about going to the cleaners, or have the students write one. Have them go over it so that they are comfortable enough to improvise. Role-play a typical scene at the cleaners, using real clothing lists.

2. Using the Yellow Pages, have the students look up names of cleaners in their neighborhood. Have them call and ask the price for cleaning a certain article of clothing. Next, compare prices at different local cleaners. Which store gives the better deal?

3. Write a price list on the board:

shirt	$1.00
skirt	1.50
jacket	2.00

Divide the class into two groups, giving each group a bagful of clothes or pictures that have been cut out of catalogues, magazines, and the like. Ask them to write up the cleaning ticket. How much would it cost to have the items cleaned? This would be a good time to discuss the reasons for dry cleaning an article of clothing rather than machine or hand washing it. You can build a separate lesson about types of fabrics. Do your students know the difference between cotton, polyester, and wool? Are they familiar with synthetic materials?

ACTIVITY 8:

Understanding Transportation Schedules *(intermediate through advanced)*

OBJECTIVES: *To learn to read timetables; to learn time telling in English; to learn the vocabulary used in transportation schedules; to ask and respond to L2 time-related questions*

The simplest way to obtain schedules would be for you to call either a train or bus depot and request them to send you enough for your class. Even more rewarding and beneficial to your more *advanced* students would be to ask them to write letters as a class assignment, requesting schedules to be sent to them at the school address.

You may think that reading a schedule is a skill all people have, and not a necessary part of ESL. WRONG! First, many students have never used a timetable in their native country. Thus, you would be providing them with a new skill they just might need in their new country. Second, transportation schedules are a great instructional source for teaching time telling. Always start with a simple schedule, concentrating on the time one would catch the bus/train/plane and the time it arrives at its destination.

Make sure the students are familiar with the words *gate, departure, arrival, a.m., p.m., peak* and *off-peak hours,* and so forth. Discuss the changes from weekday to weekend schedules. If the day is a holiday, which timetable would you use? Explain the meaning of the empty spaces on the schedule that tell the rider that there is no service at that time or place. Depending on the level(s) of your ESL students, you can do any number of related projects.

New York-Albany-Syracuse- Rochester-Buffalo-Niagara Falls-Detroit

Km	Mi			63	69	73	71	75	65	49	79
		Train Number		63	69	73	71	75	65	49	79
		Train Name		The Niagara Rainbow	The Adiron-dack	The Empire State Express	The Henry Hudson	The Washing-ton Irving	The Salt City Express	The Lake Shore Limited	The DeWitt Clinton
		Frequency of Operation		Daily	Daily	Daily	Daily	Daily	Daily	Daily	Daily
		Type of Service		☒ ⌂	☒	√ ☒	☒	☒	√ ☒	🛏 ✕ ⌂	☒
0	0	*(Conrail)* **New York, NY** *(ET)* *(Grand Central Terminal)*	Dp	8 40 A	9 15 A	12 40 P	2 40 P	4 40 P	5 40 P	6 40 P	8 40 P
53	33	Croton-Harmon, NY ⑯		R 9 37 A	R 10 03 A	R 1 28 P	R 3 28 P	R 5 28 P	R 6 28 P	R 7 37 P	R 9 28 P
119	74	Poughkeepsie, NY ⑯ *(Highland)*		R 10 21 A	R 10 48 A	R 2 13 P	R 4 13 P	R 6 13 P	R 7 13 P	R 8 21 P	R 10 13 P
143	89	Rhinecliff, NY *(Kingston)*		10 37 A	11 04 A	2 29 P	4 29 P	6 29 P	7 29 P	8 37 P	10 29 P
185	115	Hudson, NY		11 02 A	11 27 A	2 52 P	4 52 P	6 52 P	7 52 P	9 02 P	10 52 P
230 230	143 143	**Albany-Rensselaer, NY**	Ar Dp	11 45 A 12 05 P	12 05 P	3 30 P 3 40 P	5 30 P	7 30 P	8 30 P 8 40 P	9 45 P 10 00 P	11 30 P
245	152	Colonie-Schenectady, NY		12 26 P		3 55 P			8 55 P		
257	160	Schenectady, NY		㉘		㉘			㉘	㉘	
286	178	Amsterdam, NY		12 54 P		4 20 P			9 20 P		
383	238	**Utica, NY**		1 55 P		5 17 P			10 17 P	11 52 P	
406	252	Rome, NY *(Griffiss AFB)*		2 11 P		5 31 P			10 31 P		
460	286	**Syracuse, NY**		2 42 P		6 02 P			11 05 P	12 45 A	
599	372	**Rochester, NY**		4 15 P		7 32 P				2 20 A	
695	432	Cheektowaga, NY ㉘ •									
705	438	Buffalo, NY *(Central Tml.)*		5 32 P		8 40 P				3 50 A	
708	440	**Buffalo, NY** *(Exchange St.)*	Ar	5 37 P		8 45 P					
748	465	**Niagara Falls, NY**		6 40 P		9 45 P					
938	583	St. Thomas, Ont. •		9 28 P							
1115	693	Windsor, Ont. • *(Amtrak Sta.)*		11 10 P							
1120	696	**Detroit, MI** *(Amtrak Sta.) (ET)*	Ar	11 30 P							

ACTIVITY 9:

Using Can Labels *(intermediate to advanced)*

OBJECTIVES: *To become a more knowledgeable consumer; to become more aware of the product information on labels; to learn about marketing techniques; to increase and improve L2 word attack skills; to increase L2 vocabulary*

Can labels should be simple to collect from the homes of your students, colleagues, and friends. If the labels do not come off easily, they can be removed by submerging the can in warm water and carefully peeling off the label. Lay the label flat between towels to dry.

The labels that you have collected contain many words, an understanding of which is essential to being a knowledgeable consumer. (See "Preparing Consumer Education Units." See also Appendix E.) Have the students read each label and call out the items they see. Some they might find are:

1. weight or net weight
2. ingredients
3. distributor
4. size of portion
5. RDA (Recommended Daily Allowance)
6. nutrition information (calories, protein, fat, carbohydrates)
7. recipes
8. size (economy, family, trial, etc.)
9. K (kosher)
10. U (inspected by Union of Orthodox Rabbis)
11. parve (something that can be eaten with dairy or meat products)
12. instructions (*e.g.*, shake well, refrigerate after opening)

Make a list on the board and discuss each item as it comes up. Answer questions as they arise. Label reading exercises should be spontaneous and natural even in the classroom setting. Prevent them from being boring by using some fun projects. Here are a few to spark your students' imaginations:

1. Create a label for a particularly favorite food of yours. Include the information found above. Be artistic and design a new logo.

2. Invent a new food product you would like to see on the market. Design a label for your new product. Be sure to include items 1 through 12.

3. Design a COMPARISON SHOPPING CHART. Have other students fill in the chart.

SAMPLE CHART

FOOD	BRAND	STYLE	WEIGHT	PRICE
tuna fish	Chicken of the Sea	in water	8 oz.	$.79

If you have enough labels, compare three brands of the same product. Students can either complete the assignment in class or take a trip to the supermarket.

4. Provoke thought and further classroom discussion. Perhaps after the discussion, the students can divide into small groups and make posters to demonstrate the point of the discussion, *e.g.*, effective advertising, nutritional importance, food poisoning, chemical ingredients vs. natural foods.

With younger students, let them set up a store in class, using cans, boxes, containers, and so forth. Then have them prepare a shopping list and do their "marketing." They'll even enjoy trying to figure out how much they owe and counting their change. You may want to use Monopoly money for these transactions. The class can also make their own money.

ACTIVITY 10:

Learning from Vacation Brochures and Posters *(advanced)*

OBJECTIVES: *To learn how to plan every aspect of a trip; to learn about a particular place of interest; to learn how to conduct research*

Travel agencies are a great source of posters and displays to brighten up your room. Vacation brochures can be used alone or in conjunction with your geography lesson.

1. Base a lesson around a brochure by asking your *advanced* students to read its charts and answer questions about price, occupancy, extras, and special deals.

2. Have students pick and choose from the brochures to approximate the cost of a trip, including everything from choosing the vacation place to determining the type and cost of transportation. Have them itemize everything, including food allowances. They can pretend that they have traveled to their destination. Have them write a composition about what they did and how they spent their time. Did they enjoy their vacations? What a fantasy!

3. Brochures and magazines are great if for nothing more than cutting out and pasting pictures. If the students are studying a particular continent, have them draw a large outline map on an oversized sheet of paper attached to the bulletin board. Then, assign the students their own area or country to fill in with pictures that relate to the geography and industry of that particular place. Ask the students to paste the pictures on the map to form a meaningful collage. The completed project will be a beautiful work of art, as well as research you and your students can be proud of.

This might be a good time to present a how-to lesson on, *e.g.*, how to select, fold and pack clothes for a short snow-skiing trip to the mountains or a camping vacation. See "Look Who's Teaching Now," page 36, for assistance. This is a good role play situation. Discuss the wisdom of buying traveler's checks for a trip and how to use and safeguard them, if you're working with adults.

ACTIVITY 11:

Learning from Drivers' Manuals *(advanced)*

OBJECTIVES: *To learn about driving laws and customs; to learn necessary vocabulary associated with driving; to improve L2 listening, speaking and reading skills*

Students would certainly be interested in any lesson you devise from a driving manual. Always take time out to discuss the driving customs and laws in other countries. Even if your *advanced* students already take driving theory or a related course in the high school, don't be afraid to be repetitious. They may feel uncomfortable speaking in a large group of native speakers and, although they might understand, they may not participate in the discussion. Typically, in the ESL class, where they feel more comfortable speaking their new language, they will be proud to share their knowledge with their classmates. In most states, it is easy to obtain free drivers' manuals for the entire class. A related activity is the reproduction of road signs—their actual shapes, colors, and wording or drawing. We have found oak tag to be particularly suitable.

The penalties for driving under the influence of alcohol (or any other toxic substance) should be discussed here, with DWI (driving while intoxicated) initials they should never want attached to their names. Local and state laws and penalties regarding DWI, seat-belt usage, and the like can't be emphasized too strongly.

ACTIVITY 12:

Preparing an ESL Class of ________________ Yearbook

OBJECTIVES: *To learn the give and take of social interaction,* e.g., *sharing ideas and tasks, cooperating, assuming responsibility; to learn organizational skills; to follow complex directions; to meet "deadlines"; to set a long-term goal and see it through to its conclusion; to learn "real-life" publishing tasks; to display mastery of all L2 skills with a permanent record of the year's ESL program activities*

At the beginning of the year, establish the idea of the ESL yearbook. (Once you've done it, you'll have something concrete to show future classes.) Set aside an area of the room or a closet where materials can be saved that record the weeks' or months' activities and/or any special events that the class wants to record. If someone can supply a camera (you may turn out to be that someone), it would be great to have some class pictures. You may have some good photographers in the class. School yearbook pictures of seniors or pictures of their families or special events in their lives that they're willing to contribute will all enhance your yearbook. Toward the middle of the year, have them thinking about an "editor-in-chief," assistants, typists or those with word processing skills/access, and so forth. (See "Can I Have Your Autograph?" for help in organizing the technical aspect of putting this together.)

Where there are yearbook faculty advisors and an editor-in-chief for the school yearbook, these people would be good resources for the project. This type of activity encourages interaction with mainstream students in a positive and enjoyable way. For those ESL students who are not yet seniors, it provides an opportunity to develop some practical experience that might enable them to try out for the school yearbook in the future. In districts where there are sufficient funds and/or a print shop, the ESL Yearbook could be printed and distributed to all ESL students "graduating" from the ESL program and to any other appropriate individuals in the school/community. It's also terrific to have on hand when parents and other visiting dignitaries come into your classroom. The ESL Yearbook is a super culminating experience!

Successful Fund-Raising

Techniques and sources

If you question the purpose of fund-raising in ESL classes, we urge you to consider this activity not only as a money-making project but, more importantly, as an educational tool that provides a hands-on introduction to the realities of the American marketplace. Consider all the language skills the students use in planning and preparing any project. Think of all the camaraderie that is necessary to pool ideas and to work together toward a single goal. Consider their satisfaction when the event is over and they have succeeded in achieving what they set out to do. Fund-raising isn't only for obtaining money. It can be a step in developing self esteem, class unity, and individual as well as group pride.

Once you've established a need for funds (*e.g.,* field trip, transportation, scholarship fund, donation to hospital, room improvements, expensive projects), and have set a specific goal, you are ready to elicit ideas from your students. Ask them to vote for the best idea and to choose a chairperson to lead the campaign. Then, as the students begin to organize, aid them in selecting any appropriate dates and times relative to the event(s). Help them devise their work schedules. Of course, all fund-raising events must be approved by the administration, and here we urge you to use diplomacy. But whatever it takes, be positive. Remember, your students *must* have this fund raiser!

Publicizing the event is extremely important to ensure success. The amount of money and kind of fund raiser will determine the quantity and quality of advertisement you will want and the procedures you will follow. Don't hesitate to contact local newspapers and radio stations. Stir up as much excitement and support as possible within the school.

In the past, our classes have held fashion shows for which they have sewn and modeled their own clothes. Bazaars and fairs can be staged to sell handmade craft items. We've sponsored countless dances and "garage sales"; school flea markets and sales of shoelaces, pens, etc., with the school name on them are other possibilities. Why not try a children's theater performed and produced by high school ESL students? A talent night? Get parents and other teachers involved. What fund-raising activities do you and your students need? Here are some additional sources to help underwrite your program's expenses:

1. Contact the appropriate division of your district, county, state and/or federal Office/Bureau/Department of Education and inquire about free services, availability of grants and/or mini-grants, and so forth.

2. Secure a copy of the current edition of *The Annual Register of Grant Support* for information about grant support programs of government agencies, public and private foundations, business and industrial firms, unions, educational and professional associations, and special-interest organizations. This book is published by Marquis Academic Media, 200 West Ohio Street, Room 5608, Chicago, Illinois 60611.

3. Contact local clubs, especially ethnic organizations, for financial and moral support. This might be an excellent source for scholarships for your students.

4. Check with the funding officer(s) at your county or state college(s)/university for additional sources and assistance in applying for a grant. The appropriate administrator(s) in your school district is/are also a good source of practical assistance.

5. Try and find an "angel," an individual or company who is prepared to demonstrate his/her/its support by donating money to ensure the success of the program. For example, tactfully ask relatives and friends who are in a position to offer such tax-exempt financial aid for their assistance.

6. Ask for fund-raising information ideas and texts from your local, county, or college librarian. Perhaps if enough people are interested in this topic, the library might be willing to conduct a workshop on the topic.

7. Launch an ESL alumni fund-raising campaign. This, of course, is only possible if your program has been in existence for a number of years. (This is also a great source of possible guest speakers. See "Inviting guests to your classroom.")

8. Where available and applicable, involve your students in a Junior Achievement Program, a 4H Club, or something similar. These organizations help train young people in the ways of business. This knowledge can be translated into valuable work experience for the youngsters and into dollars for your program. (It has been said that if you give a hungry person a fish, he or she can eat for a day. But teach that person to fish, and she or he can eat for a lifetime.)

9. Secure permission from the appropriate school and local authorities to run a fifty-fifty raffle. This could be tied in with some special civic and/or school function.

10. Keep your ear to the ground for any financial help which might be available for your students from any legitimate source. See also "It Works" columns in TESOL and NABE *Newsletters* and *ESL Action Reporter* (by Armando Riverol; Hayward, California: The Alemany Press, 1983).

NOTE: Be sure to thank all those who have given their financial support to your students. Preparing thank-you notes can be an important educational activity for them. A word of caution: In your enthusiasm, don't assume that all of your sources wish to be publicly acknowledged. Check with them *before* you proceed.

Units for the Classroom

They've Got Your Number

Using the telephone and directory with ease and efficiency

Using the telephone as a teaching device provides several activities for your beginner student:

1. answering *yes/no* questions

2. giving information:
   a. type of phone;
   b. telephone number;
   c. resources for making phone calls outside the home.

3. increasing vocabulary, *e.g.*:

long distance	area code
person-to-person	emergency
station-to-station	speed calling
collect	call waiting
wrong number	call forwarding
information	answering machine
deposit	message units
accept the charges	

4. learning to be independent and efficient, *e.g.*:
   a. finding numbers in the white pages;
   b. locating resources in the Yellow Pages;
   c. giving and taking messages;
   d. making doctor's appointments;
   e. calling for emergency assistance;
   f. using the telephone socially;
   g. understanding phone rates and bills.

Put the words *rotary* and *push button* on the chalkboard. Draw a simple diagram of the two dialing systems. You can begin your discussion with something as pedestrian as:

1. "Do you have a telephone?"

2. "What kind of telephone do you have?"

With intermediate students, lessons can include: (1) how one obtains a telephone; (2) choosing from the various phone company services available; (3) how bills can be paid; (4) how to read your phone bill and what to do if there is a problem with the bill; and (5) how to handle obscene or bothersome phone calls. Naturally, your suggestions would coincide with the age of your students.

While this unit is essentially a unit for students at the middle school level and older, it would be wise to teach elementary school children how to use the telephone in an emergency and how to answer the telephone in English, since they are sometimes the only English-speaking persons in the family.

Before you introduce your students to this unit, call your local or regional telephone company. They all have special departments for working with schools, some under public relations, some under education, and so forth. Your local business office will connect you with the right department. Tell that person what you're up to and be prepared for all kinds of freebies, even more than you can use. Ask for however many telephone directories you need, so that each student has one. The year and county don't matter so long as the books are all the same. At the primary level, you may want to request phone books from rural areas as they are generally smaller and, therefore, easier to manipulate and follow. In large cities, you may need two sets of books, since the classified may be a separate book. Make an appointment to have the teletrainer equipment (see "Appendix C") sent to your school for a week or so, unless there's a system set up as a permanent part of your school as there is in some high school business departments.

Many students have use of the telephone as part of their everyday lives in their native countries.

1. Ask them how one answers the telephone in Spanish, Italian, and so on. Be prepared for a variety of answers: "¡Oigo!" "¡Diga!" "¿Cómo?" are just a few Latino responses we've received, for example.

2. Discuss how the telephone can be answered in English and solicit answers from students as to why how one answers the telephone is important. Be sure the class understands that *how* means more than just the word(s) used.

a. What can you tell from the voice on the other end of the line? (approximate age, educational level, sex, mood, or manner of person answering the phone)

b. Do any of the above affect you as the caller? How? (intimidation, for example, by a curt voice)

c. What does this mean with regard to the way *you* answer the telephone?

3. Discuss the importance of telephone etiquette in relation to 2.

You might want to use the following true story as an illustration of how *not* to answer the telephone:

A young Egyptian doctoral student unexpectedly arrived in the United States on Super Bowl Sunday armed with the telephone numbers of the only two people he knew in America. He called the first one. There was no answer. He called the second one.

Martine: Hi.

Caller: Hello. May I please speak to Dr. Maculaitis.

Martine: Absolutely no!

Thus, three-year-old Martine Maculaitis slammed down the receiver, dismissed the caller, took no message, and returned to the Super Bowl party. Martine's team won. The day's big loser was the young researcher who ended up spending a small fortune on hotel and food bills until he finally reached Martine's mother several days later.

4. Ask why people use the telephone:
   a. social calls;
   b. business calls;
   c. emergency calls.

5. Use the chalkboard to explain some essential telephone vocabulary, *e.g.*:
   busy signal
   collect
   deposit
   dial tone
   information
   long distance
   operator
   out-of-order
   person-to-person
   station-to-station

Blackline masters designed to streamline teaching and learning are provided at the back of the book for easy removal, duplication, and use. See Masters 1A and 1B for vocabulary for this unit.

It is essential to provide *beginners* with simple explanations. You can even use a toy telephone for showing simple dialing or push-button operations.

6. Explain *alphabetical order* and *last name first.*

   a. Put the names of your students on the board and have them alphabetized.

   b. Be sure to explain alphabetical order not only from the standpoint of last names and how to move to the second letter of each person's name when the first letter is the same, but also how to move to first names and initials when the last names are the same. Give simple examples to be alphabetized: Garcia, Rosa; Garcia, A. J.; Garcan, Mary; and so on. It's most important that students understand what we take for granted.

7. Give each student a phone book and let them glance through it for a few moments. Then, ask them how they would look up a number. Ask them to look up their own last name in the phone book and to write down what page it's on (or could be on). This will give you an indication of whether it's time to move on or whether you need to review alphabetical order again.

8. Have the class turn to the table of contents and discuss:

a. alphabetical order relating to the contents;
b. the purpose of a table of contents;
c. some of the vital information they can find quickly.

Have them find the page with area-code information. Call out different places and ask them to give you the correct area code. Next, show them briefly some of the information they can find in a telephone book besides addresses and phone numbers. (Some telephone books are bilingual; many offer first aid and emergency advice, survival guides, and services from which you can create more sophisticated units with your *intermediate* and *advanced* students.)

9. Choose five names at random in the phone books you are using and put them on the chalkboard. Ask your students to copy the exact name and find: the address, the phone number, and the page number in the directory for each one. Show them beforehand that the names at the top of each page are alphabetical clues. The page number will help you check quickly and provide you with information concerning their skills or the lack of them in this area. You can repeat this lesson again should you find there is any aspect you must reteach before proceeding to the Yellow Pages.

10. Explain the purpose of the Yellow Pages and have them glance through to see the many services they can find.

11. Suggest since they are new to the town, they might want to find a doctor. Have them look under *Doctors*. Usually, there will be a notation to see special kinds of doctors, including *physicians*.

a. You can have a short, one-sentence course on synonyms here, including very basic examples like *smart, intelligent,* and *easy, simple*.

b. Explain that *doctor* and *physician* can be synonyms and that they will sometimes find directions to look under different names for the information they are seeking.

c. Have them look for physicians and write down the name, phone number, address, and page number of one. Check the page number to see if they're in the right area.

12. Depending on the age group, suggest or have students suggest something they'd like to buy or have repaired, or some service they'd like performed. (With older students, watch your wording!) High school students, for example, usually want to buy a car and we spend some time looking for cars. "See *automobiles* . . ." They discover they can buy a new or used car, rent or lease a car, get parts for a car, have a car repaired, and so forth.

13. Tell your students your sink is overflowing, the TV is broken, you need to rent a car to get to a movie tonight, you don't know what's playing at the movies, and you have a terrible headache from the whole mess. Ask them (and help them) to tell you what to do.

a. If no one mentions it, ask them if they know the name of a plumber (write the word on the board) and be sure they know what a plumber is.

b. Following the established pattern, have them write the name, address, telephone number, and page number in the book of a plumber. Get some of their suggestions. Always have them tell the page number so others who might be having problems will see where the information is.

c. Follow the same routine for TV repairs and renting cars.

d. Ask the youngsters how to find out what's playing at the movies since you don't have a newspaper and no one is around to tell you. When they suggest the telephone book, ask the class to locate the name and so on of a movie theater and then have them find a doctor, reminding them about synonyms.

14. A fun "test" to see if students have mastered the idea of how to use the telephone book would include setting up a situation such as the above either from their suggestion or from areas that are appropriate to their age/grade level. Always have them include name, address, telephone number, and page number so you can verify. Tests should be graded and returned to them for error analysis with them.

Now that you can use the phone book with relative ease, it's time to make some calls. Since their very presence in an ESL class indicates they have come from far-away places, it is important to teach about more than local calls. With older, more advanced students, you may want to also arrange for a telelecture and/or teleconference hookup in your school. These are both powerful team-teaching tools.

1. Discuss what a local call is and how one is made from home and from a phone booth.

2. Review (it may not be review) *area code, dial tone, busy signal, hang up and dial again.*

3. Ask them if they know what "information" is, how to dial it, and that they should use it only if a local number cannot be found in the phone book and for areas not covered in your phone book.

Teach them how to dial for information. Remind them they must give the entire name, city, and if possible, address of person(s) they are trying to reach. Explain that the phone may be listed under someone else's name and, therefore, a correct address is crucial in cases where there are many of the same last names in the book. (You might want to point out the pages of Smiths or Wongs in the phone book you are using.)

4. Define the different types of calls and what they mean:

a. *long distance*—calling far away;

b. *station-to-station*—you must pay for the call if anyone answers the phone, even if the person you want to speak to isn't there;

c. *person-to-person*—costs more than station-to-station but you only pay when the particular person you have called speaks to you;

d. *collect call*—the person being called pays for the call (See "making calls");

e. *operator*—dial 0 in case of emergency. Tell the operator what the problem is so he or she can notify the proper authority and the name and address where the emergency is occurring. Be sure to emphasize the necessity for *clarity* and for giving the *city* as well as the street and any apartment number where the fire, fight, or illness is occurring.

f. *credit card calls*—if you belong to a particular telephone company that offers its own credit card telephone service, you can apply for a telephone credit card from that company. If you are approved, you receive a card with your own special account number. Directions for charging telephone calls are on each card. You are charged every month for the calls you make with your credit card. Using a credit card is usually more expensive than dialing direct.

g. *800 numbers*—there is no charge for calls to 800 numbers. These are usually business numbers.

Making Calls: Role-Playing with or without Phones

If there is no teletrainer to be had and there are no similar facilities in your school, use toy telephones or your imagination, and have students turn their backs to each other and practice making these types of phone calls:

a. emergency;
b. information;
c. doctor's appointment;
d. long distance person-to-person;
e. collect call;
f. wrong number;
g. message (party not there).

You might want to start by being one end of the conversation in each case so the student will get an idea of what information to elicit or impart in completing the calls and conversations.

Have all your students get a turn at role playing each situation and be sure there's lots of time for conversation from them about what was left out or what needs to be included in each type of call and proper etiquette, *e.g.*, "You told the operator there was a fire on Main Street, but you forgot to say what city" or "The receptionist asked if you could come in at 8 P.M. and you work nights. Suggest a time that's better for you." or "You forgot to dial the operator to say you want to speak to Mary Jones person-to-person. If you don't tell the operator, the call is station-to-station." These are excellent listening activities too, in very natural situations.

A final test might include:

a. role-playing a particular type of call;
b. matching vocabulary and definitions;
c. finding names and services in the telephone book and listing appropriate information;
d. having your students fill in the missing words in the sample dialogue which follows:

Patient: Hello. This is ________________ . I want to make ________________ appointment with Dr. Patel.
Nurse: Can you ________________ in at 7 o'clock tonight?
Patient: ________________ , I can't. I work. ________________ can come in tomorrow ________________ 4 o'clock.
Nurse: 4 o'clock is good. ________________ do you spell ________________ name?
Patient: ________________________
Nurse: Fine. We'll see you ________________ at 4 o'clock.

With an *intermediate* group, a quick review will show you what they know and don't know about all of the above. After any review you feel is necessary, ask the students if they have a telephone, and if so, how they arranged for it. What did they (or their family) do? A sample lesson might include the following words:

ads, advertisements	installation fee
card	jack
check	money order
classified	obscene
disconnected	out-of-town
exchange	plug
extension	receipt
harrassing	receiver
install	temporarily

Discuss: (1) how one orders a telephone; the fact that while various phone styles provide the same service, some are more expensive than others; (2) questions one should ask when applying for a telephone, *e.g.*:

a. How much will it cost?
b. What are the monthly charges?
c. Are all phone styles the same price?
d. Are all colors the same price?
e. How much does it cost for more than one phone?
f. Does it cost less if our phones are all installed at the same time?
g. Is there a one-time charge or a monthly charge for more than one phone?
h. Is it more economical to buy the equipment or to rent it?

(3) methods of making payment; (4) checking bills and saving receipts; (5) deciding *before* the installer arrives where you'd like the telephone(s); (6) being sure someone is home when the installer is coming; (7) asking for I.D. of the installer. How your number is listed in the telephone book is also important. You might want to use the phone books to show the students various listings. Ask how *their* phones are listed; for example, are they listed in *their* names? Why or why not? Unlisted or unpublished numbers should also be mentioned, including the fact that it costs money *not* to be listed. Let them discuss their own experiences with obtaining a phone in this country, and if they have something interesting or unique to tell about telephones in their own country, leave some time for that, too. You might want to invite someone from a local telephone company to come in to speak to your students and to answer any questions the class might have. You might also want to arrange for a field trip if there is a local or regional training center where your students can see not only the complicated process set in motion when they pick up the receiver, but also the variety of job skills employed by a telephone company. This, in itself, can provide future lesson plans when discussing careers.

With *intermediate* and *advanced* students, especially in the upper grades, it would be appropriate to discuss how to handle obscene or harrassing phone calls. Use discretion in discussing these types of phone calls with very young children.

The amount of role-playing and the numbers of ways you can use the material in the telephone book are endless. (For example, ESL/EFL students like publishing their own class telephone directory. The directory pages can be run off on a duplicating master or copying machine.) You can spend days just on the table of contents. Many phone books now have bilingual components, and you might want to point that out. You can really go a long distance with a great deal of free material and imagination.

Making Tomorrow's Career Begin Today

A comprehensive unit plan for grades K–6

Grandmother: What are you going to be when you grow up, Beth?

Beth: A nurse.

Grandmother: A nurse? Why not a doctor?

Beth: Only mens (sic) can be doctors.

Grandmother: Women can be doctors, too. And men can be nurses.

Beth: Well, anyway, I'm going to be a ballerina.

(This is a transcription of an actual conversation between four-year-old Beth Scheraga, a professional model, and her Grandmother Mona. Beth's mother and maternal grandmother also work.)

Recognizing that destiny is not merely a matter of chance, but, more significantly, a matter of choice, now is the time to talk about developing appropriate strategies for helping young children participate in the choosing and preparation of their vocational destiny. *High school is too late to begin career education.*

Our favorite career quote is "A foolish consistency is the hobgoblin of little minds," courtesy of Ralph Waldo Emerson. In dealing with career exploration at *any* age, the first thing we tell our students is they have the right, the option, and the opportunity to change their minds, not only during initial vocational exploration, but even after working at a career for years. There are innumerable examples of people who have done this. Isn't it just as important to find out what we are *not* suited for as it is to find out what will make us happy and successful? And since the more sophisticated of us know that being successful and rich does not necessarily mean being happy (otherwise, what are we doing in teaching?), values sorting is a vital part of career exploration.

This guide (and it is meant only as a guide) can be adapted for native speakers of English and for older learners, although it was developed primarily for high *intermediate* to *advanced* ESL students in the elementary grades, kindergarten through six. You can and should make suitable adaptations for the particular grade level and students you're teaching.

Major objectives are:

1. to have students think about themselves as individuals who:

a. have desires, dreams, goals;

b. are able to achieve said desires, dreams, goals;

c. are able to pursue the proper steps toward achievement of their goals;

d. are free from the prejudices of sexism, racism, and other biases affecting career goals;

e. are able to deal intelligently with prejudices of family, friends, etc., should they involve undue influence in career choices (overtly or covertly).

2. to have students realize they can and should be free to change their minds as they mature. (We must stress again that students should be made to feel they needn't be locked into a decision made at age six should they find at age sixteen, or sixty their ideas, needs, goals, and so forth, have changed.)

3. to stimulate curiosity and awareness.

4. to have children realize that the more they know, regardless of the source, the more intelligent choices they can make, and the more able they will be to evaluate the relationship between their goals and their own makeup, emotionally, physically, intellectually. Realistic choices can better be made after one examines and tests her or his capabilities. Over the years, we have all heard teachers at one time or another snicker as they repeat the hilarious story of a Karl, or Carol, classified educable, who says he or she is going to be a doctor. We must encourage children while helping them to find their own realities. This leads to objective 5, *i.e.,*

5. to have students able to appraise themselves at appropriate levels and to develop a heightened self-awareness.

6. to help students, many of whom have already been defeated, unconsciously, by sex, age, race, ethnic, religious or socioeconomic stereotypes, to realize they *can* rise above these stereotypes to pursue their goals once they have been shown how.

7. to involve parents; to make them aware of their children's thoughts about their own futures so that students, teachers, and parents can work together. (This may involve a separate session or two with parents, many of whom may seem a bit surprised that such young people's thoughts about the future could or should be taken seriously.) Perhaps this new respect for young people might close the proverbial generation gap a little faster. Cultural attitudes might take a little longer, depending on various socioeconomic and historic factors. One thing is certain: parents are not made unhappy by teachers who are genuinely concerned about their children.

8. to make guidance counselors aware that:

a. ESL students can fit into many mainstream programs if they have a special interest and the ability; *i.e.,* art, journalism, music, and so forth;

b. they must ask students what they would like to do in the future and really *listen* to the answers so they can be guided accordingly.

Methods for developing career or vocational awareness in the elementary grades would include a great deal of discussion: discussion of how the students see themselves (if they see themselves at all). The teacher has to make them aware that they are more than physical beings—that they are creative beings with the capabilities of generating strategies for success and controlling, at least to some degree, what happens to them in the future. Children must be taught that they *can,* or at least that they *can try.* If they try and don't succeed . . . ? We must give our students the courage to try again, benefiting from their experience and using new strategies.

How much sadder to spend our lives wondering what we might have been or could have done than to have had the experience of trying and perhaps not achieving all that we set out to do. How many techniques and methods of teaching ESL or EFL have we all experimented with before hitting on those that work best for us with particular students? We must translate our own risk-taking efforts to our youngsters in ways that are meaningful to them: "If you don't try, you'll never know *what* you are capable of, whether it's learning to ride a two-wheeler, learning to speak another language, or making a dream or two come true."

A good technique for image building is to have students look for the *positive* characteristics in their classmates. Vocabulary would have to be appropriate to age, grade, and language level, of course. A suggested opening might be for the teacher to go around the room and tell one nice trait or mannerism that she or he sees in each child, explaining first that each person is a unique individual with certain physical, mental, and emotional characteristics. She or he might mention Juan's smile or Josef's good manners or Maria's speaking first to the new student in the class, and so forth. Then the ESL teacher asks each child to tell one *nice* trait about the child next to him or her (to ensure that each one hears something nice about himself or herself). It will be enlightening to see what the youngsters consider positive traits. The way Alex clicks his gum or Sandra fills out her sweater may not be what *you* had in mind, exactly, but then it isn't *your* mind that's being explored. This leads right into values sorting. (See Sidney B. Simon, Leland W. Howe, and Howard Kirchenbaum, *Values Clarification: A Handbook of Practical Strategies for Teachers and Students.* New York: A and W Publishers, 1978.) Again, depending on the age group, you can ask what is meant by *values.* In grades where students can read, you might want to write their responses on the board. If you seem to be the only one who knows what a value is, don't be shy: explain. Then ask them what some of *their* values and beliefs (perceptions) are. If your students name their bikes or baseball cards and material possessions only, you can lead them gently into "whom" they value and some of the values they may not yet recognize as such, *i.e.,* happiness or health. Eventually these values will reflect their perceptions about themselves and their future possibilities and will be related to career choices. Below are some practical suggestions for beginning discussion on careers, including a clarification of the meaning of *career* itself.

Begin discussion of careers

1. "What is a 'career'?" Elicit responses. (See Masters 2A–2B for grades 4–6.)

2. "What's my (the teacher's) career?"

3. "What's *your* career now?" (After answers, or no answers, suggest being a student is a career; "Your value of that career plus other factors will help to make you the kind of student you are.")

4. "What's another name for *career*?"

5. "Can you name some careers?" After the obvious,

> **a.** *suggest* some others they might not think of—housekeeper (avoid sexism whenever possible), parent, other health-related careers besides doctors and nurses;
>
> **b.** *discuss* the fact that all jobs and some hobbies can lead to a career—one must begin somewhere . . . the principal was a teacher first; owner of a store may have started as a sweeper; their favorite movie or TV star may have started as a dishwasher (a few actual examples add credibility to your statements);
>
> **c.** *talk* about prejudice—some people think only men can be mechanics, only women can be nurses . . . "What do you think?" Discuss how lucky they are to be young today when people are finally beginning to understand that women can be architects, doctors, firefighters, etc., and that men can be flight attendants, nurses, homemakers, etc. "Some people will never understand this, but we'll deal with that later."

6. Why do people work? Discuss. Another opportunity for values sorting. Money is not the only satisfaction to be had from working.

Bring in a montage; talk about what a montage is and how it's made. Suggest to the class that they might want to make a career montage to hang in the room. They can cut out pictures from magazines (which you may have to provide), draw their own pictures, or bring in photographs of people at work (a parent, a friend, and so forth). You can all hang the background paper along the wall or wherever circumstances permit, and generate much talk and anticipation about this new project that is not only *by* them but *about* them. You can show them pictures from current texts. See References. In relation to the montage, the ideal situation would be to encourage your students to arrange it themselves in their own way. Each day, as a new crop of pictures is drawn or hung (and the pace at which you do this is again based on your judgment as well as practical considerations), each career should be analyzed as it is placed in the montage. For example, you might ask, "Can a man and/or a woman do this job? Why or why not?" If you get only a "no," show why either sex can, in most cases. Ask "Can a person of any race or ethnic background have this job? Why or why not?" Clarify for the youngsters. Be sure they know the meaning of *race* in this context, and of *ethnic background* and *prejudice*. Be sure *you* know the meaning of these words. If and when you see their prejudices coming through, it's extremely important to try to reach them right then and there! Discuss prejudice: what it means and where it comes from; how no one wants to be discriminated against but how they, themselves, may be acting with prejudice toward others. Show them how one can be prejudiced *for* or *against* something or someone, perhaps using their own parents' automatic defense of their children's behavior when speaking to the teacher or principal, or *your* prejudice about how special your students are when you brag about them to other teachers.

When reading and writing skills permit, you and the class could make a class booklet or job kit of your own, listing jobs, their requirements, salary scale, and benefits, with pictures or drawings of someone at the job. You might even have a "come as your future vocation" day. Take pictures of the students with slide rules, microscopes, stethoscopes, shorthand notebooks, violins, tape measures, calculators, chef's hat, or whatever, to be entered in the booklet. Our all-time favorite career-related anecdote happened when another teacher's student came to school dressed as a shepherd—and indeed, he went on to become a shepherd, in Australia. And how we had laughed at what we thought was his humor that day! Some examples for discussion might center around what is needed to become a shoemaker, entertainer, electrician, welder, secretary, teacher, or some other jobs that they might suggest, and how one goes about preparing for these careers. It is very important for them to understand that tomorrow's career begins today, and that their reading, writing, and computing skills build foundations for success in and out of school.

It should be clear by now that a very important component of a career unit is values sorting and the individual's belief system. Respect for each person's job is essential. In many cases, our students' parents fall into job categories that some second- and third-generation Americans turn their noses up at; *i.e.,* building superintendent, garbage collectors, streetsweepers, unskilled laborers, and so forth. If you've ever been in New York City during a sanitation workers' strike, your nose probably turned up for another reason. Ask your students questions such as "What happens when the police go on strike? What would happen if nobody wanted to be a garbage collector?" They must be educated to see that everybody's job has value, and we must count on each other to carry out our responsibilities if society is to advance and prosper.

The easiest and most interesting way to teach respect for and stimulate curiosity about various jobs is to tap human resources in the community. In general, we have found people to be flattered by the invitation and eager to share their expertise with young people. In fact, they love it, and the kids love it, and, perhaps even more significantly, it brings the school closer to the community and the community closer to the school. It is particularly important to find people of ethnic and racial backgrounds similar to your students' to come in and talk about their jobs and to demonstrate, where possible, a product they've created or worked on. Also, if possible, introduce a male and a female who have the *same* occupation, *e.g.,* flight attendants, police officers, postal workers, nurses, and so forth. Finding bilingual resource people who use both languages on the job: department of immigration personnel, court interpreters, individuals in international or multinational corporations, hospital workers, probation officers, and so forth, is extremely helpful in *showing* students the value of knowing more than one language and the kinds of job opportunities available if they are truly bilingual. For the more ambitious teacher, where feasible, you might want to bring in a media person to tape or film the class and its project for a local TV or radio program or have the local newspaper do a pictorial essay of the project. In line with this, you might arrange free or inexpensive field trips to a local TV studio, radio station, hospital, newspaper, city hall, police station, and so forth to let children see for themselves the myriad jobs involved in running these types of establishments. A trip to the supermarket would show them not only clerks and cashiers, but also such employees as stock people, secretaries, buyers, outside salespeople, and the like. What an eye-opener to discover the various types of jobs in a newspaper plant or hospital, from maintenance to management, from receptionists to researchers!

Students can keep adding to the montage while at the same time building a personal vertical file with their vocational materials, including an individual career log and their latest self-assessments, as they expand their career exploration from grade to grade and career orientation programs become more sophisticated. As they mature, as many avenues of career exploration as possible should be investigated. Make sure the students cover areas such as professions, public service, service areas, media, skilled and unskilled labor, sales, entrepreneurs, armed services, social services, professional athletics, and fine arts professions in their personal vertical files.

During this process, it might come as a surprise to them, if not to you, to discover that some plumbers currently make much more money than some lawyers and that if a student *really* wants to be a doctor, she or he had better be prepared to spend four years in college, four years in medical school, three years in internship and residency, and so forth. And if show biz is their dream, they must be prepared for years of hard work and "pounding the pavements" before they are finally "discovered," if they ever are, that is. They must learn to cope successfully with the possibility of failure. That is a difficult lesson to teach as well as to learn, but the only *real* failure is in *not trying*. In the meantime, it would be useful and kind to teach them the wisdom of having a second career "in the wings."

Classes should include talking about the results of each day's homework assignments, *i.e.,* discussing the day's events in relation to their work on careers with their parent(s) or guardian(s) or some member of their family who is concerned about their future. Students should get their suggestions and help, whenever possible. They should be encouraged to ask family members and friends about their jobs: Are they happy with their work? Would they like to change jobs? How did they find their jobs? If they could do any kind of work they wanted to, what would they do? Why don't they try for that goal if they are not doing that work now? Some good discussions can be generated at home and in the classroom, with children: learning the realities of being locked into a job if one is lacking in certain skills or education; being brought closer to their families through meaningful interaction; helping to strengthen the ties between home and school; letting mama or papa have her or his "moment in the sun," encouraging their children to become all they are capable of becoming.

Each day you can give a different child a chance to discuss what they talked about at home in relation to careers.

Active parental involvement in the education of one's child or children *is* essential, at times even crucial, especially in the formulation of attitudes and the sustainment of motivation.

We suggest that at the beginning of this project a note be sent home to parents (in the native language if necessary, and if possible) telling them briefly about this unit, what you are planning to do and why, and asking them to work with you and with their children toward the beginning of career exploration. You can tell them they will be invited at a later date to a Parents' Day where they will see some of the results of this new and exciting unit and the influence they, the parents, have had in helping their children think about their futures. When the time comes, invite the parents in. Have the students help in planning for a Parents' Day. Discuss who will do what job, what jobs they think are necessary for planning the day, being sure somewhere along the line that someone suggests writing invitations, planning a program, having a student MC, ushers, refreshments (if desired), and so forth. An invitation can be laid out on the chalkboard for each child to copy, inviting the person(s) of his or her choice, or there can be an invitation committee based on handwriting and reading skills (You're putting your unit to work already!) or whatever you deem most appropriate for your class. Each child *must* have a job related to Parents' Day, including seeing that the room is in order, doing a bit of interior decorating, planning for and obtaining refreshments, serving, cleaning up afterwards, hosting and/or any of the several other jobs you and they discover must be done. Don't be surprised if you have to do another values-sorting exercise should you see that no one or only a few volunteer for the unglamorous jobs such as cleaning up after the event. A program committee, or the class, should decide how this special day is to be conducted; *e.g.*, setting up a schedule for:

- **a.** who will explain the career montage;
- **b.** how the booklets will be displayed and discussed;
- **c.** who will obtain and who will serve refreshments;
- **d.** how introductions of parents to the teacher, other students, and other parents will be done;
- **e.** who will entertain questions from the parents;
- **f.** what type of evaluation of the project should be done by students and parents;
- **g.** how much time should be allotted for each part of the program.

At your Parents' Day, explain to the parents what you tried to do in this unit, including stimulating the youngsters to think about their futures, to purge themselves of prejudice, and to realize the importance of school in helping them reach their future goals. Do seek evaluation of the project from both parents and students. This evaluation may be as formal or as informal as you wish.

Perhaps the hardest, yet most revealing, part for you, might be making a serious formal evaluation for yourself. (See Masters 12A–12B.) Was it worth the time and effort? Did you reach at least *some* of your students? Did you all have some fun? Would you do it again? If not, why not? What changes can you make so that your answer will be *YES* next time? Don't take "no" as a final answer—especially from yourself!

Making Tomorrow's Career Begin Today

A comprehensive unit plan for grades 7–12

For those students who are uprooted from their native environments during their adolescent and teenage years, it is particularly important to make the "new" language work for them so that they will see purpose in working toward learning it. (Again, this unit can be adapted for the adult education learner.) High school may be their last chance, or the beginning of a new chance.

1. Let the students themselves talk about who they are, what they really like and dislike, what their concerns are, what they would like to do with their lives, and how to convert their dreams into reality:

- **a.** What are their goals?
- **b.** What attributes will help them?
- **c.** What obstacles stand in their way?
- **d.** How do they think they should attempt to achieve their goals?

2. Discuss the current job market, the changes taking place, preparation for the changes, values and how they affect career choices, prejudices and how to deal with them: in essence, every aspect of the emotions, beliefs, and attitudes involved in career decisions.

3. Talk about the right and wrong ways of job seeking, sexism, education, manners, and the lexicon involved in discussing careers intelligently.

See Masters 5A–5B for vocabulary for this unit. Students can look up definitions and/or write them in after class discussion.

A Sample Lexicon

applicant	laid off
application	overtime
benefits	perks
company policy	personnel
employee	qualifications
employer	references
employment agency	resumé
FICA	salary
fired	service fee
handicaps	social security
hired	union
interview	withholding tax
interviewee	any words students
interviewer	ask about

4. Consider:

a. The advantages and disadvantages of employment agencies:

1. the rights and responsibilities of everyone involved;
2. signing papers *after* reading and understanding, dealing with pressures.

b. how to deal with the pressures associated with job hunting, including practical application of what has been learned.

5. Teach them how to:

a. prepare a simple resumé;
b. fill out an application blank (see Masters 7A–7B);
c. answer an ad by telephone and by letter;
d. go for an interview;
e. ask the right questions;
f. play the game;
g. put their best foot forward, and so forth.

6. Discuss their prejudices (yes, we all have them) and how to cope with their own as well as those of others.

At times, reality and how to deal with it need to be stressed, as well as constant reinforcement of positive thinking. The instructor must constantly keep in mind the destructive force of the self-fulfilling prophecy and encourage the student to perceive ultimate success in long-range terms based on daily input. *Perseverance* and *guts* become two very familiar words.

Talk with your students about equal employment opportunities, equal pay for equal work, how they feel about these concepts, cultural and generation gaps in career planning (many of the girls face the problem of parents who don't see the need for a college education) and how to cope with them, knowing how to be a successful test taker, the changing job market and how to fit into it. The students should be taught how to write a letter of application for a job and a letter accompanying a resumé. Have them bring an ad from a newspaper or magazine and answer it, including addressing the envelope properly. They should create their own basic resumé and fill out actual applications which they have brought in from local factories, supermarkets, stores, and offices. You can also have on hand applications from colleges, national franchises, airlines, and the like. Students then have the opportunity to discover they are not yet spouses, have never been bonded or refused bond, and are in the position of being asked to respond to many questions they legally no longer have to answer. State and federal laws should be discussed with them. They must be encouraged and permitted to decide individually whether to answer the questions asked and perhaps get the job, or refuse to answer on legal grounds and perhaps get turned down. Whatever their decisions, no value judgments should be expressed, at least intentionally, by the instructor, and an attempt must be made to present *all* sides of a situation.

An important step is a class trip to the school library, where the students can research the career they're interested in. Skills necessary for using the library efficiently, organizing and writing a paper in English, and investigating one's future are all involved. Before the trip, a career inventory should be given each student and should be thoroughly discussed, especially the reasons that an inventory is needed, and what the results might show. (How much better to find out *now* rather than after years of study and preparation that this career is really not what one thought it was, not really what one would enjoy doing.)

Career Inventory Sample (see Masters 6A–6B for actual use)

1. Title of job being investigated
2. Qualifications needed
3. Experience needed
4. Starting salary
5. Prognosis
6. Availability
7. Drawbacks and handicaps
8. Self-analysis
   - **a.** What I need to qualify for career chosen
   - **b.** My present qualifications and experience
   - **c.** Can I live on the salary offered?
   - **d.** Is the job worth it?
   - **e.** Am I willing to relocate if necessary?
   - **f.** Does my personality suit the job?

g. Is there prejudice to be faced in the career with regard to sex, religion, race, age? Can I cope with it?

h. Do I have the stamina, drive, and equipment to deal with the emotional, physical, and mental demands of this career?

i. How can I achieve this career now that I have decided I am suited for it?

OR

What have I learned about myself? Where do I go from here?

Students should understand that a starting salary and the prognosis for advancement in a career are both important. Either the instructor or the librarian can give the students a mimeographed sheet of career possibilities. (See Federal Register, *Annual Occupational Outlook Handbook,* Washington, D.C. United States Department of Labor, Bureau of Labor Statistics, current issue.) These can be investigated in the careers section of the library with the help of the instructor and the library staff. The students should have their career inventories with them so that they can begin to seek the necessary information. We suggest at least a week for preparation of the written paper, with adequate time for discussion of any questions they might have and for showing them the form you want used. This is also a good time to reinforce the habit of proofreading their work before submitting it.

It is desirable, too, to have resource people who are actively pursuing various careers of interest to the students come in to talk with the group and answer their questions. In addition, ESL students should be included with mainstream students for any high school career days. Here, students can ask questions about several different careers in one day. For some, this is the start of thinking about the career options open to them. Get involved in the National Junior Achievement Program available through your state. See References and Master 4.

The variables and the economic changes that have occurred in the community over the years should also be discussed. Changes in government spending and automation cannot be overlooked. Students are encouraged to take advantage of every available opportunity while constantly reevaluating themselves and their values and goals. One of the most rewarding experiences comes when their concepts of the exciting jobs available in certain industries are discussed. For example, they know about pilots and flight attendants; however, most are unfamiliar with the many related employment opportunities connected with airline work. Of course, doctors and nurses work in hospitals, but students are surprised when the possibilities connected with health careers, such as dieticians, technicians, aides, maintenance personnel, switchboard operators, secretaries are discussed. Expect the buzz in the room to become louder as each student tries to come up with another possibility.

It is an eye-opener, a vocabulary builder, and it requires a noisy session or two to find out how many different kinds of jobs are involved, whether it's putting together a newspaper, getting an item of clothing ready for sale, or even running a school. Where can one find one of these jobs? Various resources are discussed: classified ads, radio, TV, employment agencies, footwork, friends, signs, and so forth. Attention should be paid to the pros and cons of using employment agencies and of knowing how to ask the right questions, especially *before* signing any papers. Stress should be placed on the proper form for writing a business letter, the importance of checking with people *before* using them as references, and the importance of neatness and accuracy in everything one does.

At the end of these activities, students are ready to be interviewed for their jobs. Again, every facet of a successful interview needs to be reviewed.

Students need to be reminded of appropriate dress for a job interview, including acceptable hair styles/lengths, clean fingernails, and suitable attire for the job/organization. Since even the most astute interviewer may be unsophisticated about the mores and behavior of other cultures, body language can be easily misread. Therefore, it is necessary to review those aspects of acceptable, expected American behavior and social patterns that might affect their success potential: shaking hands firmly (practice shaking hands with each member in class and have them shake hands with each other, boys with boys, boys with girls, etc.), maintaining a reasonable amount of eye contact with the interviewer (we don't mean a hypnotic stare!), answering questions so that the interviewer perceives the job seeker as someone who really wants the job, is qualified for it, or is willing to do whatever is necessary to become qualified, who will be an asset to the organization, personally and professionally.

Use sample questions and model good and poor answers, letting them decide *why* one answer is better than the other, *e.g.*,

Can you type?

Yes.

Can you type?

Yes, I can type 60 words per minute.

Can you type?

No.

Can you type?

No, but I'm willing to learn (or, I'm very determined; I could go to night school, etc.)

Go over the interview from its inception, telling them to wait for the interviewer to speak first, to invite them to sit down, to begin the questioning. Remind them to sit up straight and to avoid nervous mannerisms. If the interviewer gives them a chance to ask any questions, they should ask those questions they still have relating to the job description, work schedule, salary, opportunities for advancement, etc., before they ask about benefits, "perks," and the like.

At the end of the interview, regardless of the outcome, they should shake hands with and thank the interviewer.

Those who have already experienced job interviews can relate their experiences and answer other students' questions. In addition, advice should be given on the graceful way to ward off sexual overtures as well as the necessity for coping with the unexpected, including being offered a job other than the one originally applied for. Then each student should choose a partner to work with, each pair compiling a list of appropriate questions to ask the other. The pairs will work in front of the class, switching roles of interviewer and interviewee, and should assess their partner's ability to perform each role. After the interviews have been completed, and the prospective personnel have been "hired" or not, the entire project can be evaluated by the group. The best evaluations are those in which the students come back from actual interviews with job offers they feel they would not have received otherwise. In two specific recent instances, an opportunity to be trained for a better job than the one applied for was possible because the interviewers were so impressed with the students' poise and enthusiasm.

Such fine results make this a particularly satisfying unit. It forces use of ESL and survival skills: the students are improving their English, enriching their vocabularies, using their imagination (while, we hope, thinking in English), participating actively in real-life roles as job seekers, sharing information with their families (you cannot translate the target language into your native language if you do not know the target language well enough), and learning to make *their* destinies *really* theirs. Again, specific textbooks are not necessary. However, the increasing number of excellent books dealing with career exploration can make the instructor's task an easy one. The "References" contain some, but by no means all, of the current career texts on the market.

Making the System Work for You

Tenants, leases, landlords, and the like

Here's an exciting project that cannot be started too early. The elementary ESL student may be the only one in the family who can communicate well in English and must serve as the family interpreter and spokesperson. What follows is exactly what we did. Try it; it's up for adoption.

The majority of the junior and senior high school students who participated in this experiment are immigrants, primarily from Latin America and the Caribbean. The next largest groups are from India and Poland. They live, for the most part, in urban situations. Housing problems are familiar to all, especially the problems of roaches, absentee landlords, unlighted hallways, faulty locks, and sanitation deficiencies. That these problems have always existed in the community, as in most urban areas, is noted. However, students are informed that there are laws to protect tenants as well as landlords. Their rights and responsibilities as tenants and/or landlords and working within the legal process are also discussed. A sample lexicon includes:

absentee landlord
addict
apartment
attic
corporation
deposit
derelict
eviction
exterminator
flat
fluorescent
hazards
insurance
interest
landlord
lease
liability
litter
mortgage
plumbing
receipt
rent
responsibilities
rights
rodents
rundown
security
slumlord
sublet
superintendent
tenant
tenement

(See Masters 8A–8C for vocabulary for this unit.)

The pros and cons of leases, reading and understanding a lease before signing, not being afraid to ask questions, realizing that a lease is a contract, getting receipts for any cash given are also mentioned. A typical first-day discussion might include talk about where they live, whether they rent or own their apartment, flat, or private home. The problems of finding a suitable place to live, leases or the absence of same, security deposits, painting, rats and roaches, all are discussed. It is not unusual for each student to have a problem that causes another student to talk about a similar experience. Clearly, the utilization of the target language could not be more meaningful. An inspector from the local housing authority might be invited to talk to the students and to answer their questions. For example, salient points of the local building code could be explained to them as well as their rights and responsibilities as tenants and/or landlords. Perhaps they could be told how to file a complaint with the housing office and discuss the violations that might turn up in housing inspections of their premises. (Because of the thoroughness with which the experimental group of students had approached the subject, the chief of inspectors chose to return twice to the classroom and turned the findings about the students' understandings of and interest in the subject into a news article for the local newspaper. Naturally, the students were delighted to read about themselves in print, something they could not do if their English weren't improving.)

On the day that the building inspector visits your class, the students should have their home inspection sheets with them. Their survey can be divided into three columns for each item: *satisfactory, unsatisfactory,* and *comments.* A sample housing inspection checklist:

HOUSING INSPECTION FOR (ADDRESS OF PREMISES)

(see Master 9)

Item	**Satisfactory**	**Unsatisfactory**	**Comments**
I. Exterior			
A. Sidewalks, fences, immediate surroundings			
1. free from litter	____	____	__________
2. in good repair	____	____	__________
3. sufficiently well lit where indicated	____	____	__________
B. Outside brick, paint, and so forth in good repair	____	____	__________
C. Doors, windows properly secured: locks in good working order	____	____	__________
D. Garbage disposal areas			
1. sufficient covered areas for disposal	____	____	__________
2. area clean and free from infestation	____	____	__________
3. adequate garbage collection to avoid overflow	____	____	__________

Item	Satisfactory	Unsatisfactory	Comments
II. Interiors			
A. Communal hallways, stairwells, areas			
1. properly lit	____	____	____________
2. free from garbage and litter	____	____	____________
B. Paint in good repair	____	____	____________
C. Mailboxes properly secured	____	____	____________
D. Exits not blocked by carriages, bicycles, litter	____	____	____________
E. Fire escapes working properly and free from litter	____	____	____________
F. Easy access to fire escapes, all exits (special stress in this area is necessary because of frequency of fires in many older buildings)	____	____	____________
III. Individual premises			
A. Sufficient heat and hot water	____	____	____________
B. Plumbing in good order	____	____	____________
C. Sufficient electrical outlets	____	____	____________
D. Outlets working properly	____	____	____________
E. Stove in good working condition	____	____	____________
F. Paint in good repair: no peeling, no lead paint, no holes or leaks	____	____	____________
G. Landlord abides by state law - *(e.g.,* in some states, tenant is entitled to free paint job every three years.)	____	____	____________
H. Apartment is free from infestation: adequate extermination control (In New Jersey, a new tenant in an apartment is entitled to a paint job, free of charge, extermination service, and a municipal inspection before moving into the apartment, that is, as of this printing.)	____	____	____________

The findings are discussed with the building inspectors, who will probably offer practical suggestions for correction and assure the group they cannot be harassed or evicted for complaining about violations. Students must be told the precise legal method for making a housing complaint, beginning with a friendly discussion about the problem(s) with the superintendent, then with the landlord;

next, putting it in writing and following up after a proper period of time with complaints to the Housing Inspector's office. You should also teach them about the existence of and services rendered by the Small Claims Court and the Legal Aid Society, as this information may prove necessary. Unfortunately, most people are easily intimidated. In the circumstances, we believe in the teacher's responsibility to educate students concerning their rights, responsibilities, and recourse. (See Appendix D for additional sources of assistance with a housing problem.)

A sense of understanding and recognition usually emerges with the people and situations read about in daily newspapers and popular magazines and seen nightly on television newscasts. Complaints of insufficient heat, poor plumbing, no hot water, eviction notices are commonplace. The other side of this is often a revelation to the students: landlords are people, too. Seeing your property constantly vandalized is expensive—financially and emotionally. You can get some good discussions going about owner and tenant responsibility.

Be sure to discuss whether building codes work (if not, why not?) and subsequent legal action—fighting back through tenants' organizations and the courts.

From the stories presented, from their own surveys and experiences, each student can be asked to choose a problem of special concern. Then, individuals with common problems can work in groups, each group having a judge, a lawyer for each side, a landlord, and a tenant, with the rest of the class serving as the jury. Each group would present its particular case to the judge and jury. The interest and professionalism displayed by the group in producing its own courtroom drama will make the instructor's preparation for the unit worthwhile. It is of particular interest to note that as a result of their readings, discussions, and inspections, the jury might *not* always decide in favor of the tenant. Because they now recognize the rights and responsibilities of each person, each case will be judged on its merit and on the evidence presented. Students practice their new language, utilize their knowledge of the American judicial system (with no small thanks to TV), and learn about survival in the new culture, while having fun. You might want to invite a local judge to sit in.

Preparing Consumer Education Units

Now that your students have a job and a place to live, they will have some serious shopping to do. *Caveat emptor.* You should discuss everything from flimflams (there is at least one a week written about in the local newspaper) to bait-and-switch techniques. Teach them how to do various kinds of comparison shopping, read labels for fiber or food content, understand truth-in-lending laws, and what the word *interest* means when we are paying it rather than receiving it. Discuss packaging, the psychology of advertising, the subtle power of words, especially the word *only,* sex appeal as the hidden premise in everything from car purchases to dish detergents. Talk about soft sell and hard sell and let them discuss specific commercials that have influenced them and try to analyze why. Talk, too, about what brands of specific products they or their families usually buy, why they buy certain items at all, where they buy them and why. (A version for elementary school students can begin with comparison shopping of bubble gum brands and getting the best deal on trading cards.) The benefits and drawbacks of credit cards, of shopping in department stores, supermarkets, and neighborhood stores are essential parts of the investigation.

In conjunction with the readings (see References), advertisements, and commercials, the class learns about the many different ways it is possible to be cheated (fraudulent mail order schemes, door-to-door salespeople, subscriptions without end, unauthorized or unsolicited materials sent to the home, and so forth). Talk about recourse through Small Claims Court, the Legal Aid Society, the Department of Consumer Affairs, the Better Business Bureau, local, state, and federal law, especially concerning the mail. Train them to ask for and save receipts, to avoid sending cash through the mail, to realize the wisdom of using a money order instead.

A sample lexicon can include:

consumer
comparison shopping
Caveat emptor
Better Business Bureau
Office of Consumer Affairs
Legal Aid Society
Small Claims Court

defendant
plaintiff
collection agency
loan company (finance company)
loan shark
interest

usury
illegal
swindle
bait and switch
chain referral
consolidation loan
credit certificates

(continued on next page)

(continued from previous page)

advertisements
commercials
degrees of truth (indirect lies vs. direct lies)
lay-away plan
installment plan
charge
down payment
balance
bargain
installed
warranty, guarantee
contract
bill
truth-in-lending
shrink
faded
summons
cheated
risk
fair price
manufacturer
limitations
sales trap
unsolicited
goods
hard sell vs. soft sell
sales pitch

(See Masters 10A–10D for vocabulary for this unit.)

Begin with questions such as:

a. Do you shop with your family?

b. Where do you shop? Why?

c. Do you shop for your own clothing?

d. What brand of coffee (rice, beans, juice, chicken, and so forth) do you (your family) usually buy? Why?

e. Did you have to buy furniture when you moved here? Did you shop around before you bought? Do you usually shop around?

f. Are you influenced by TV commercials? How? Are they expensive to produce? Who pays for them? Do you and I?

While the discussion period is still alive with a feeling of discovery, assign each student the task of bringing to class an advertisement from a newspaper or magazine which can be discussed from the standpoint of the hidden message, the type of sales pitch, loaded words, and so forth. Next, the students should be divided into small groups to discuss each other's ads and then present their final findings to the class. Each student can then create an ad or commercial for an imaginary product or an imaginary brand of an existing product, working alone or with other class members. They will do their own art work, decide on a sales pitch, write a script or prepare some other method of presentation. They might prepare an ad for a newspaper, a magazine, or a radio or TV commercial. Obviously, a discussion about what is necessary to be effective in each of these media would precede actual production. This will prove a valuable lesson in itself. As each ad or commercial is presented, the student audience should note why they would or would not purchase the product on the basis of what they heard or saw. The presenter would tell what he was trying to accomplish and how. (If TV and recording equipment are available, it is extremely useful to record the presentations for playback. Here is tremendous opportunity for self-correction, ego-building, and fun.)

From the influence of advertising, proceed logically to stories in various texts, newspapers, and magazines chronicling various types of sales traps: bait and switch, chain referral, dishonest door-to-door salespeople and home repair services, and the omnipresent con artists, who are particularly adept at swindling those who have difficulty with the dominant language/culture. You will find that almost everyone has an experience to share that has happened to an uncle or a godmother or the lady next door. Discussion of loans is of primary importance, too. Where to borrow, what to know before borrowing, understanding the truth-in-lending act, avoiding loan sharks and why, should all be part of the discussion.

Familiarization with consumer rights is very important. There should be instruction in: knowing what to do if one is faced with a situation where he or she doesn't want to be switched from the bait; the meaning of time payments and the actual interest charges involved; how to utilize a warranty properly; being careful not to be pressured into signing anything whose meaning is not clear. An assortment of free publications in English (and many in Spanish) available free from the U.S. Government Printing Office may be distributed for home consumption, so that the students can assist their families. (See References and Appendix E.) They should be taught that no matter what they receive in the mail, if they did not order it, they are not responsible for returning it, acknowledging it, or paying for it; companies and charities cannot expect unsolicited goods to be returned or paid for by the recipient. Stress should be placed again on not signing anything that is not *completely* understood. Teach them to request and, if necessary, demand identification which can be verified of persons who claim to be officers of banks, policemen, and so forth. They must be told that collection agencies are not allowed to harass. At this point, a detective and/or lawyer might speak to the class, even more than once, because there are so many questions to be asked and numerous experiences to be recounted. (The speakers inevitably turn out to be as eager to return as the students are to have them back.) In every community there must be several untapped human resources, who often speak the same native language as your students, who would be eager and flattered to be invited to offer their expertise. (See "Inviting Guests to Your Classroom.")

Another session should be spent in a discussion which would include the various acts and laws protecting the knowledgeable consumer: Pure Food and Drug Act, Fair Packaging and Label Act, Wholesome Meat Act, Wool, Fur, and Textile Labeling Laws, Truth-in-Lending Act, to cite just some of the necessary-to-know legislation.

Students are quick to learn the wisdom of prescription comparison shopping, of seeking another doctor's opinion when one doctor recommends surgery, and asking a doctor's fees before, not after the examination. By the time they are ready to do their own comparison shopping, the final project in this unit, they will know how to read the labels on cans, boxes, and so forth, what the order of ingredients listed means, and that *meat flavored* is not the same as *meat.* They will know that *economy, super-economy, giant,* and *family size* are names with psychological rather than physical value—the ounces tell the real story. What they see is not necessarily what they get.

When the students finally go out to do their own comparison shopping, they will have two kinds of shopping to report on in class: Compare the same product, same brand and quantity, in two different stores; and compare the same product, same quantity, two different brands in the same store. Students record the names of stores shopped, date of shopping, brand names and quantities, types of containers, and prices. Each student will report his findings to the class. To avoid duplication, each student should choose a product to compare ahead of time. Regardless of what is selected to compare, the method must be the same. The classroom should be enlivened by the exchange of findings and the honest shock of discovering sometimes substantial price differences on two items with identical contents but different brand names. Students should also bring in ads from local newspapers and comparison shop in class, evaluating coupon offers among other things. Shopping centers, supermarkets, discount stores, and neighborhood stores should be evaluated for prices, convenience, service, return policy, and so on. The students should be allowed and encouraged to draw their own conclusions. Throughout the experiment, the role of the teacher is that of a catalyst or facilitator, one who helps students develop into intelligent consumers, through knowledge as power. By the time you are finished, the students, who often have participated actively in family shopping expeditions, will be showing off their expertise in comparison shopping. Generally, the unit ends with the decision that a little suspicion, a great deal of knowledge, careful thinking before one acts, thoughtful weighing of alternatives, and knowing where to turn if one suspects she or he has been cheated are all necessary components of a competent consumer.

“Can I Have Your Autograph?”

Developing and improving writing techniques

Writing, like many other language skills, progresses from the simple to the more complex, from the personal to the academic or technical. For most students, including those for whom English is the native language, writing is never simple. We can't let this defeat us—or our students. Teaching writing, especially from the standpoint of skills building, is probably the most frustrating task for ESL teachers and learners. There's frustration right here with exactly how to begin this section.

Journal writing has become one of the most effective methods of eliciting and encouraging natural writing at all levels of English proficiency. It is a “free” writing experience that frees both student and teacher, since there is no evaluation of any sort. The focus is on the relationships that develop through journal writing: the relationship between student and teacher and the relationship between the students and their inner thoughts. The student finds it progressively easier to transcribe thoughts and feelings to paper. Once exposed, these thoughts and feelings are responded to in a nonjudgmental way by the teacher, who never comments on or corrects grammatical, syntactical, or spelling errors or makes value judgments on the thought processes or beliefs of the students.

The teacher gets a clearer picture of the students and, from a cognitive standpoint, can plan together with them where they should go from here. Students learn that they can express themselves on paper, can become more responsible for improving their vocabulary and writing skills, and have a trusted friend in the teacher who really cares about them and what they have to say. With the tension eased, what once was a formidable task, writing in any form, becomes something to look forward to.

Begin by explaining what a journal is and how it's going to be used in your class: as a private communication between you and the student. Talk about getting started, the hardest part for many people, even professional writers. Offer some suggestions:

“Start by writing the date. Tell me about something you saw (on television, in the school cafeteria, in the newspaper) or heard (on the radio, from a friend, in the street). Maybe you'd like to write about your past, what school was like in your native country, how you felt when you first arrived here. Perhaps you'd rather think about the future. What are your plans? Tell me what makes you happy, angry, sad. What embarrasses you? What hurts your feelings? How do you feel about keeping a journal? Write about anything or anyone that comes to mind.”

Once they get started and then read your responses, the connection is made, affectively as well as cognitively.

Arrange for an accessible but private (secured) place in the room to keep your students' journals (which can be notebooks or several sheets of paper stapled together with a place on the outside for their names). At the initial experience, pass out the journals, tell them to write their names on the outside and show them where they'll be kept. Allow at least ten minutes for the first journal entry, then schedule a specific time slot for each meeting.

At the beginning of each class session they're to take their book and begin writing. At the end of the allotted time, collect the books or have a student do so and be sure they're where they're supposed to be for the next session. The number and length of your responses to their writing will depend on your personal time constraints, the size of your class, how many classes you teach, and how many times they meet each week. At the beginning, even a sentence or two of response from you is important to keep the flow going. As students read your thoughts and feelings on the subject they've written about, they will be encouraged by the knowledge that they're corresponding with someone who cares about what they have to say. This accelerates the writing process on all levels as self-confidence and positive self-images are stoked by the mutual involvement of journal writing.

In line with the concept of learning by doing and by patterning correct models, let's continue with *dictation,* a technique for all proficiency levels. We have found, through trial and error, that one of the most successful methods of teaching correct sentence building through dictation is to "routinize" the monthly dictations. It helps, also, with learning numbers and which months have how many days. On the first school day of each new month, for example, we begin with, "This is the month of ____ . There are ____ days in ____ ." Students look forward to this as something comfortingly familiar and are soon beginning the dictation for us, an unexpected reward we have now come to listen for after the first three months' dictations.

Dictation is a most effective device for: (a) improving listening skills; (b) analyzing errors; (c) imparting information; (d) increasing vocabulary; (e) providing material for discussion; and (f) building foundations for good writing through examples. A dictation for *beginners* might include material about any holidays or vacations for the particular month, a change of seasons or clocks. For example, in those areas where clocks are turned ahead for Daylight Saving Time, that month's dictation might look like this:

This is the month of ____ . There are ____ days in ____ . Before you go to sleep Saturday night, (date) , be sure to turn your clock *ahead* one hour. You will lose an hour's sleep that night. In the fall, you will turn your clock *back* one hour. Remember: "Spring forward, fall back."

Among the other various types of dictation are:

a. meaningful dialogues;
b. questions and answers;
c. paragraphs;
d. poems;
e. brief news items.

(For those of you who want to know the readability level of prospective dictation material, see Edward Fry, *Fry Readability Scale,* Providence, Rhode Island: Jamestown Publishers, 1978.)

Methods for giving dictation vary. One we have found to be most successful involves part of three class sessions.

DAY 1

Put the dictation on the board or use the overhead projector. Have students copy. Afterwards:

a. check their work and correct any copying errors;

b. discuss vocabulary and meaning of paragraph;

c. talk about the affective, *i.e.,* do they have Daylight Saving Time (or, in October, Halloween; February, Valentine's Day, and so forth);

d. tell the class you are going to give them the dictation to write next class session;

e. suggest methods for studying/practicing.

(When available, use an overhead projector to illustrate specific linguistic skills. It allows for a clearer presentation and gives the ESL student a better view visually and intellectually of the particular area being illustrated. Be creative, *e.g.,* use colored pens or block-out squares to focus attention on specific points.)

DAY 2

Give same dictation as in Day 1. Be sure to:

a. set ground rules, *e.g.,* no interruptions during dictation;

b. read entire paragraph first *before* they write anything down;

(If you really believe people should take dictation from someone speaking at a "normal" rate of speed, as we were taught in the early days of ESL, think about why shorthand was invented; or better yet, try being on the writing end yourself. Let's be realistic and fair.)

c. read in word groups, repeating each word group once, then repeat entire sentence;

d. have students look at their corrected original dictation from the last class and have them correct any errors in today's work;

e. check each one's corrections.

DAY 3

Give the dictation test. Be sure to:

a. follow steps 2a, 2b, and 2c;

b. collect, correct, and return all papers promptly.

How you choose to mark the dictation can affect future results, especially with younger learners. High expectations from the very beginning seem to lead to quick mastery and fewer errors so that by the third encounter with a dictation unit few, if any, students will fail, and most will tend to receive A's and B's (an A being no more than two errors of any kind).

While exercise books provide means of teaching correct punctuation, spelling, word order, noun-verb agreement, and the like, we have found all too often there seems to be little application of what has been "learned" to the students' own writing. For those students who tend to be less concerned with accuracy, there is a need for constant reminders to apply to one's own writing what has been practiced in exercises, and to proofread. Motivation can come from the teacher via praise or criticism, good marks or poor marks, and all the "tricks of the trade" the creative teacher devises to stimulate a desire for achievement and a sense of self-pride. In the last analysis, however, the real motivation and final drive come from *within* the students. We have all known those students who respond positively toward good grades, for example, and vow to do even better next time, and some others who see high marks as an opportunity to slide. Therefore, we feel that while the stimulus must come from the ESL teacher, the quality and desire for output *has to* come from the student. This quality will often be directly related to the rapport and understanding of mutual goals between instructor and pupil.

What are some of these goals? They should include:

1. improving writing skills, particularly in:

a. punctuation—appropriate use of period, question mark, comma, semicolon, quotation marks, capital letters, and so forth;

b. spelling—including hyphenating properly at the end of a line, and syllabication;

c. correct use of tenses.

2. learning to organize thoughts in sequence by knowing how to:

a. prepare a simple outline form and discuss what its purpose is;

b. write a rough draft;

c. proofread, correct, and rewrite;

d. copy corrected work carefully;

e. proofread final edition for clarity and correctness.

3. instilling pride through improvement of writing skills and accomplishment.

4. encouraging desire and ability to express oneself on paper, including the realization that organized writing develops from organized thought processes. As one author so succinctly put it, "Writing with a plan is the best way, Man!" (Maurice Pillsbury, "Organized Writing Will Get You Your Tenure, Señor," unpublished essay, January, 1981.)

A student's writings also provide another medium for *error analysis* and for future lesson planning (when—went; he have; he assisted in the party). (See Masters 11A–11B for sample writing practices.) Other objectives might include the opportunity to work individually with students as they write, to help them with sentence structure, grammar, and elimination of any inhibitions restricting their "putting it on paper."

A final objective might include something permanent in print to share with each other, as well as family, friends, administrators, and colleagues. This type of project has the added advantages of having students:

a. share in a social experience and have the responsibility for "publishing" a collection of their work;

b. decide a theme, layout, artwork, and so forth;

c. learn about delegating duties and become aware of what is necessary to complete the project;

d. use artistic, typing, and clerical skills;

e. use the target language meaningfully and with increased confidence and mastery;

f. leave the class at the end of the semester or year with a collection of their own works, conceivably autographed by each "author" as a permanent remembrance of the ESL class;

g. leave behind a book or books that will be useful to the next crop of ESL learners and will be a fine addition to the ESL library;

h. establish a bank of positive experiences to draw on for future success.

Just Write for the Occasion

While topics and titles for booklets should be decided by the students, some suggestions from you might ease the burden, help organize them, and get things moving smoothly. We have been successful with "My First Valentine's Day," "My First New Year's Eve in America," "What It Means to Be __(name of student)__," "How I Felt My First Day in My New School," and the like. Some materials to have handy include appropriate bilingual dictionaries, picture dictionaries, a standard English language dictionary appropriate to the grade level, "scratch" paper, lined paper, ditto paper if you are planning to mimeograph, a stapler, typewriter (if possible), typing paper, and construction paper for a cover (or whatever the class deems suitable).

When it comes to learning language, our students are *not* blank sheets of paper on which *we* are the first to write. Therefore, as you give a dictation, they will be able to see, for example, how capitals and simple punctuation are used in English. The names of each punctuation mark and terms used in writing should be reviewed from time to time in context. Words such as *capital, question mark, quotation marks,* and the like should be familiar to your *beginner, intermediate,* and *advanced* students, and their correct applications should be within the confines of these students' writing experience. Learning not to divide one-syllable words seems to be one of the harder lessons in academic life and one which is quite fascinating to observe. How many compositions have we all marked with *does* or *word* gleefully divided with the *d* or the *w* at the end of the line and *oes* or *ord* beginning the next?

Before beginning any major writing, the following concepts should be discussed and understood:

1. the purpose(s) of the dictations ("What did you learn from taking dictations?")

2. the purpose(s) of the blackline masters, where, *e.g.,* they were instructed to change first person to third person, present to past tense, combine two sentences into one, and so forth. (See Masters 11A–11B.) ("What changes did you have to be aware of when you changed from present first person singular to third?")

3. the main thought (Have them give you an example from a recent lesson. This and the following concepts can be elicited from their dictations, from stories read, current events discussed, radio or television programs *they* choose to talk about, or any series of events they are interested in.)

4. the sequence ("What does *sequence* mean? When you write about something that happened to you, what part does sequence play? Why is it important?")

5. the paragraph and the development of the topic sentence. ("How do you know when to begin a new paragraph?" Or conversely, "How do you know when to end the one you're working on?")

6. the organization of thoughts through simple outlining. ("Many of you are thinking about going to college in the future. Some of you will take jobs or go into the military service. Applications for schools, many jobs, and the services ask the applicant to write something about himself or herself. This is called an autobiography. Pretend you are going to write your autobiography. Where would you begin?") Teach simple outline. (At least two or three class sessions should be devoted to teaching this important skill. Outlining can be used with any subject that requires an essay answer. Students should be told of the usefulness of this practical skill.)

7. the hows and whys of using an English dictionary. ("If you aren't sure of the spelling of a word in English, how can you find the correct spelling in a dictionary?")

Once you feel these concepts are sufficiently operable, you can switch the emphasis from the technical to the creative aspect of writing, your long-range goal being the aforementioned collection of students' works. (The time required for this project depends on group size, maturity, and per class time allotment each day/week.)

A. Linear Method

1. Have the class choose a theme. (Remember, you may have to feed them ideas through leading questions.)

2. Tell them to write down everything on the theme that comes to mind without too much concern about the mechanics.

3. Have them organize their random thoughts into a simple outline. (For demonstration purposes, you might want to go through this writing process yourself, beginning with your own simple outline.)

4. Teach them how to "flesh out" the outline in a rough draft. (At this point, the mechanics they have mastered should be evident. Now is the time to work with the students individually, helping them to follow their outline, to revise and rephrase, and to offer any writing assistance *they* ask for.)

5. Have them write a final draft and proofread it together.

B. Bubble Map Method

As an option to more traditional linear outlining (See "Setting Up the ESL Classroom: PLAN C"), you and your students may want to try Bubble Mapping, a fun technique for all ages which taps the brain's right hemisphere. This approach is frequently useful to creatively "free" those students who may be suffering from temporary or seemingly permanent "writer's block."

1. Together, choose a theme.

2. Print that theme in a central position on the board and circle it in colored chalk. Use this particular color only once.

3. Have each student contribute a word related to the theme. It can be any part of speech. Let the students write their words on the board or tell you where on the board you should write them. (Some psychologists believe cursive writing is more "memorable.")

4. Using different-colored chalks for different word groups, *e.g.*, red for adjectives, encourage the students to tell you which words should be circled in the same color.

5. Have the learners come up and connect the satellite bubbles to the main theme in the appropriate colored chalk. (For example, all words circled in green should be connected in green to the main theme.)

6. Choose one of the color groups and, together, construct a cohesive paragraph on the board, using those words.

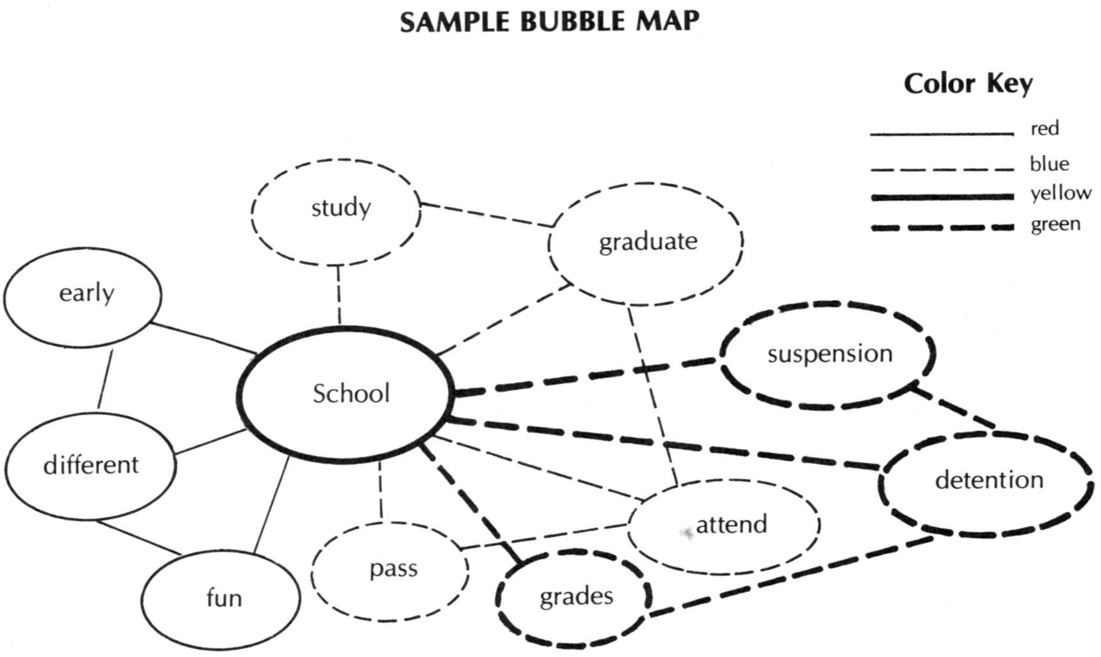

I attend school in the United States now. I come to school everyday. I study very hard because I want to pass my courses. I want to graduate.

This method of organizing thoughts and processing information should be an option for those students less comfortable with and less successful with the traditional linear outlining approach. Students can easily learn to create their own Bubble Maps on *unlined* sheets of white paper for use in the content areas where they can process information quickly through color coding, *e.g.*, in history, math, and science. It is especially helpful for many students learning the grammar and usage of another language. Coding further by shapes is also useful. Bubble Mapping can be developed to as sophisticated a level as you and your students wish to carry it.

C. "Publishing"

1. Let a volunteer typist with good skills type the story on ditto paper. (If you are without a typist, have each student copy his or her work onto ditto paper and proofread it carefully. Use primary typewriters with very young learners. If you have word processor facilities, this would be an ideal time for those with computer and word-processing skills to put them to use.)

2. Teach students how to use a ditto machine; have volunteer "printers" take turns running off the pages of the manuscript. If you have Xerox or other multi-copying facilities available, or if there is a school print shop that will do the work or allow your students to do it, so much the better. What a wonderful opportunity for team teaching and for an introduction to the school's facilities for your students. It's also an opportunity for other teachers to see your students' seriousness of purpose and to want to recruit some "new blood" into their courses.

3. Have volunteer artist(s) design a cover for the booklet that is in keeping with the theme.

4. Teach class how to collate; have everyone participate in collating and stapling.

5. Include introduction by teacher with an "Acknowledgments" page, if one is appropriate.

6. Have each person autograph his or her own work in others' booklets when the project is completed.

7. Discuss and evaluate the experience with the students.

Why not have your students improve their writing skills by corresponding with *pen pals?* They don't have to be in *Advanced* ESL to have one, but it sure helps when two nonnative English speakers try to communicate in the target language, regardless of their positions on the globe.

After the TESOL Convention in Mexico, one of our classes corresponded with a class from Guatemala. Another group wrote to students in an American business college in Japan. You might try this, using local affiliates as resources. It's easy to do!

STEP 1: Two teachers meet and decide that it would be terrific to have their students exchange letters for practice in realistic writing and for obvious educational and cultural enrichment.

STEP 2: These teachers ask their students what they think of the idea of having pen pals of their own age in Japan, Chile, Nigeria, Canada, Colorado, or wherever who are also learning English as a second language. Teachers are careful to ask the questions rhetorically so that students' only possible answer is an enthusiastic yes.

STEP 3: Next, the students will address the first batch of letters to "Dear Pen Pal."

a. Show them simple friendly letter form and etiquette.

b. Discuss some things they'd like to include and make some sort of outline on the board, *i.e.,*

---

address
date

Dear Pen Pal,

My name is __________ *. I'm from* __________ *,* and so on.

Sincerely,
Name of Student

---

c. Be sure they write about hobbies, future plans, any pets they might have, likes, dislikes, and so forth. (Your students might have questions about their future pen pals, about whom you should have some general information from the other ESL teacher. This is another opportunity for organizing thoughts, expressing themselves, practicing their English grammar and spelling, and having an enjoyable social experience.)

STEP 4: Following the above suggested outline, your students will write a practice copy of their letters. (Correct them individually for reproduction on unlined paper.)

STEP 5: Each student is now ready to write and proofread the finished letter(s).

STEP 6: At this point, the students should be shown how to fold the letters properly. Tell them you'll mail the first batch of letters with a suitable cover letter. (Our school paid for all postage since it was a school project.)

STEP 7: When the letters arrive from the pen pals, each student will be given his or her letter(s).

a. Let them read their letter(s) to the class.

b. Tell them they can answer their letter(s) on their own and begin a correspondence with their new friend(s).

c. Save the stamps for discussion.

A variation on this approach is having your students write to famous people. What a thrill when these well-known persons write back! It is also very altruistic and mutually beneficial to have students write to local nursing home residents and senior citizens. At the elementary level, children can participate in the exciting *Weekly Reader* Writing Pals Program. (For information, contact Editorial Director, *Weekly Reader,* 245 Long Hill Road, Middletown, Connecticut 06457 (203) 638-2400.)

Classes at the elementary level also enjoy sharing classbooks—being class pen pals. It is an effective way to develop and encourage communication between native and nonnative speakers.

No group is a more fertile source for stamp collecting than an ESL class. Many students or their families receive mail from their native countries and are often avid stamp collectors. You can have several different types of activities, depending on grade level, class size, and your own time pressures. For example, you might want to:

a. have students bring in stamps for a class collection which can be mounted between 8″ × 10″ plastic sheets and hung on the bulletin board or put into some kind of album.

b. form a stamp club or committee which would be in charge of collecting and displaying the stamps, with allotted time segments for discussion about various stamps, their origin, and significance.

c. create lesson plans around the various stamps, depending again on grade level, second language competency, and so forth.

Fun end-of-year activities might include:

** YOU MAY BE A PRIZE WINNER **

ESL BALLOON LAUNCH FINDER'S FORM

name of finder ______ age ______

address of finder ______

where balloon was found ______ date ______

how it was found ______

PLEASE RETURN FORM ASAP TO:

name of student ______ grade ______

school address ______

THANK YOU.

** YOU MAY BE A PRIZE WINNER **

** YOU MAY BE A PRIZE WINNER **

** YOU MAY BE A PRIZE WINNER **

1. a *balloon launch*, where each student completes a special finder's form, rolls it up tightly and inserts it into a colorful balloon provided by the teacher. Have them inflate, knot the ends, and tie their balloons with a long ribbon "tail." On a warm but windy day, everyone goes outside to the designated area. At a signal, the students release their balloons into the air. The student whose finder's form is returned from the farthest distance from the school wins the "grand prize." (The person who finds the winning balloon also would get a special prize.) All sorts of other prize categories are possible. All finder's forms that are returned are then shared with the rest of the class(es). How proud your students will be as they read the return letters and forms from the persons who have found their balloons! Of course, some balloons don't get farther than the school grounds; some may not even get that far. The real excitement lies in the possibilities and anticipation engendered by this type of activity. As in life, the anticipation is often greater than the reality. There's much to be gained in giving your students something unique to look forward to.

This is a perfect all-school activity, too. What a great way to find pen pals for your students and to generate excitement about writing and reading in the new language! *Weekly Reader* also sponsors a nationwide *Weekly Reader* Balloon Contest. Your school could win a $500.00 prize.

2. something as old-fashioned as *autograph books,* where students can write a few personal lines, a joke, or whatever in each other's homemade or commercially produced autograph books. The possibilities are limitless, regardless of age or grade level. Even primary students can draw a little picture and write their names, feeling a part of something special and permanent as they do so.

Notetaking: It's More Than Just Writing

ESL/EFL students from junior high school to adults will significantly improve their active listening, speaking, reading, and writing skills by using one or both of the following notetaking strategies.

In the *Cornell System,* have your students do the following:

1. Fold a sheet of notebook paper in half vertically.

2. Write *Main Ideas* at the top of the right-hand column and *Triggers* at the top of the left-hand column.

3. Jot down the main ideas of the lecture or discussion in the *Main Ideas* column, leaving a line or two between the entries.

4. Write down recall cues (trigger words or phrases) for each idea, lining up the entries in the two columns appropriately.

5. Cover up the right-hand column and reconstruct the main ideas from memory, using only the recall cues in the *Triggers* column. (This step should be done *as soon as possible* after the lecture or discussion.)

In the *REAP System,* have your upper-level students do the following:

1. Divide two separate notebook pages as illustrated below.

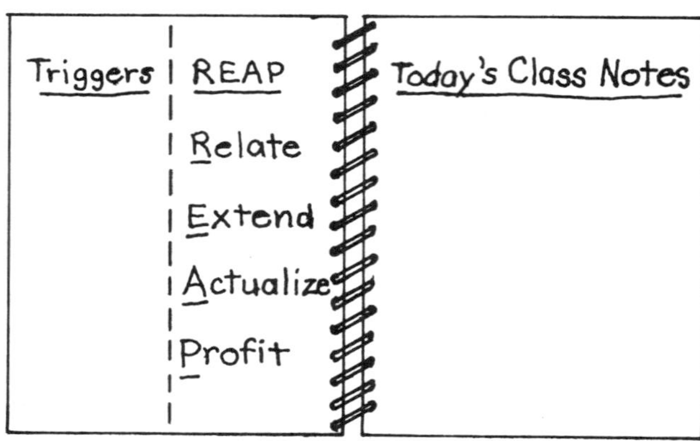

2. Take notes on only the right-hand page, using short sentences and leaving a blank line or two between each complete idea.

3. In the *Triggers* column on the left-hand page, jot down any word or phrase that triggers each idea listed under *Today's Class Notes*. (This should be done *as soon as possible* after the presentation.)

4. Use the *REAP* column to note any words or phrases from the lecture that are personally relevant. These personalized internal anchors help learners to

- **a.** *relate* the material to their own lives,
- **b.** *extend* the material to the "real world" outside the classroom,
- **c.** *actualize* the content by listing the possible applications of the material to the students' world(s), and
- **d.** *profit* affectively and cognitively.

These two trigger strategy systems can easily be adapted for making speeches, taking notes on written material, writing compositions, and reviewing for tests. When used for any of these purposes, the Cornell and REAP Systems will greatly enhance students' proficiency in all four major language skills. These ideas are based in part on the work of Walter Pauk, *How to Study in College,* second edition (Boston: Houghton Mifflin Co., 1974).

Conclusion

Probably every ESL teacher comes to the same conclusion at some point . . . "I've been teaching *X* number of months or years, and there's still *so* much to learn and do!" For most, each lesson plan gives birth to other ideas; the end of one unit is but a stimulus for the next.

We have tried to offer you not only lessons and units, but also ways of dealing with "the total student," from seating arrangements to parental and community involvement in education. We have tried to focus on solutions rather than problems; to make the learner aware that an *active* role in one's education is an essential; to show cultural diversity and nonstereotypic roles and ways to deal with the problems these ideas may generate in the minds of those ESL students for whom these options may be incomprehensible and represent true "culture shock."

The dictionary defines *elegance* when applied to ideas as "neat and simple." In this context, we hope we have given you an elegant book with which to bring even more elegance into your classrooms. Elegance transcends fashion, style, and manners as they are usually thought of. It brings with it a sense of harmony; it heightens the senses and the intellect at the same time that it makes the learner *truly* at ease in the learning situation. To this end, *E*legance *S*erves *L*earners (and teachers, too).

We hope that *The Complete ESL/EFL Resource Book* has been the very catalyst for generating your own innovations. It is important to note that the blackline masters have been designed as collateral material for this book and as a critical spark for igniting joint creative ventures between teachers and students, partners in quality education.

Appendices

APPENDIX A

PTS: Partners in Quality Education

In an effort to begin to document the growing interdependency among parents, teachers, and students (and the overall community), Dorothy Rich, founder and president of The Home and School Institute (HSI), and her staff have identified several basic principles essential to successful PTS programs. (Dorothy Rich, "Building Good Home-School Relationships," in *Today's Education,* Washington, D.C.: National Educational Association, February–March 1981, 68GE–69GE. See also Willard McGuire, "Teacher Suggestions on Parent Involvement," in *Today's Education,* Washington, D.C.: National Education Association, April–May 1981, 9G.) These principles are:

1. Parent participation is most widespread and sustained when parents view their participation as directly linked to their children's achievement.

2. The best programs provide ways for families to work with their children at home, for many parents cannot attend in-school meetings.

3. Parents like being involved in their children's education at *all* levels.

4. Programs that schools view as legitimate activities and as integral parts of the schooling process are best for building good relationships.

For additional information about HSI, write to: The Home and School Institute, Special Projects Office, 1707 H Street, N.W., Washington, D.C. 20006 or call: (202) 466-3633.

Clearly, we must all work together *before* our students' abilities become disabilities, or worse. The emphasis should be on what we can do together, on the many PTS resources that are available.

Below is a list of materials you can use to help improve PTS relationships in your community. We suggest that before ordering the following material, you contact the NEA Distribution Center by phone to ascertain availability, price if ordered in quantity, additional shipping and handling costs, and the like.

NEA Distribution Center
The Academic Building
Saw Mill Road
West Haven, Connecticut 06516
phone: (203) 934-2669

1. BOOKLET—*Parents: Active Partners in Education* by Mary Lou Sayler (0596-1-OJ) $2.00

2. CASSETTE TAPE—*Talk . . . About Parent Involvement* (0595-3-OJ) $9.50

3. FILMSTRIPS—*Parents and Teachers Together (for the Benefit of Children)* (0592-9-1J) $28.95

—*Sharing a Lifetime of Learning* (0607-0-OJ) $18.50

4. HANDBOOK—*Parent Involvement in the Schools* (1502-9-OJ) $3.95

5. LEAFLETS—*Get Involved in Your Child's School* (0600-3-OJ) Pkg. of 25, $2.25

—*Public Information Brochures* (5100-9-1J) Set of 25 different brochures, $3.75

6. RESEARCH REPORT—*Parenting* by Kevin J. Swick and Eleanor Duff (1047-7-OJ) $1.00

APPENDIX B

Sample Welcome Booklet

Spanish/English Welcome Booklet

NOTE: Please keep in mind that this sample welcome booklet is essentially the work of the students, with corrections in the native language done by other available native speakers of the language.

Aquellos que hace por lo menos un año de estar aqui, quisiéramos sugerir algunos "puntos" que esperamos le sean de ayuda a ustedes.

Now that we have been here at least one year, we would like to suggest some "pointers" that we hope will help you.

Sugeridos por:
Suggested by:

Libia Arias
Luis Barbosa
Marlon Cantor
Elvine Chomorro
Fred Conde
Alfredo Echevarria
Felix Echevarria
Rafaela Guichardo
Eladia Hernandez
Kenia Mañaná
Juanita del Orbe
Cesar Quinto
Denisse Taveras
Marta Toro

Con la asistencia de:
With the assitance of:

Mona Scheraga
ESL Teacher
Passaic High School

Traducido y pasado a máquina por:
Translated and typed by:

Delia Murphy
Bilingual Teachers' Aide
Passaic High School

Consejos Generales

1. No tengas temor de ir a la escuela. Asegúrate de tener todos tus documentos (de escuela, de vacunas, papeles de inmigración) en orden, para que no pierdas tiempo. Si no tienes los documentos apropiados, no te dejarán ingresar en la escuela. Si no tienes los documentos de la escuela te atrasarán un año.

General Advice

1. Don't be afraid to go to school. Be sure all your papers (school records, vaccination records, immigration papers) are in order so you don't lose time. If you don't have the proper records, they won't let you start school. Without school records, they may have to put you back a year.

Vocabulario—Vocabulary

profesor(a)	teacher
consejero(a)	guidance counselor
enfermero(a)	nurse
estudiante	student

2. Llega con tiempo a la escuela y a cada una de tus clases. No faltes mientras te sea posible. Pórtate bien y atento en las clases, especialmente en la clase de inglés. No tengas temor de repetir algo, aún si los demás seríen de ti. No tengas temor de hacer preguntas o inquirir por el significado de alguna palabra que no entiendas.

2. Be on time to school and to all your classes. Don't be absent often. Behave well and listen in class, especially in English class. Don't be afraid to repeat something, even if the rest of the class laughs. Don't be afraid to ask questions or the meaning of a word you don't know.

3. Esfuérzate, haz planes para una buena carrera y toma los cursos que corresponden a la misma. No pierdas tiempo. Manten todas tus anotaciones en orden. Prepárate bien cada día para tus clases con tus cuadernos, libros, plumas, y un diccionario bilingüe. Si quieres aprender un nuevo lenguaje, tendrás que sacrificarte y poner de tu parte. Si tienes un poco de tiempo libre, coje un diccionario o una enciclopedia y verás que es una buena forma de aprender a leer un lenguaje. Saca una hora todas las noches para estudiar.

3. Put forth self effort. Plan a career and take courses for it. Don't waste time. Have all your notes well arranged. Be prepared for school each day with notebook, books, pens, and a bilingual dictionary or an encyclopedia and you'll see it's a good form of learning to read any language well. Set aside an hour to study every night.

Mas vale prevenir que tener que remediar.
El respeto al derecho ajeno es la paz.

4. Aprende el abecedario en inglés. Trata de buscar información sobre los Estados Unidos: sus costumbres, geografía, etc. Cualquier cosa que puedas aprender será mejor que nada. Aprende las costumbres de la escuela. No te sientas mal ni te pongas nervioso cuando los muchachos americanos se rian de ti. Trabaja fuertemente y aprenderás. Evita que te pongan en clases atrasadas por que no sepas el lenguaje.

4. Learn the English alphabet. Try to get some general information about the United States: its customs, geography, etc. Whatever you learn is better than nothing. Learn the customs of the school. Don't feel bad or get nervous when you see that American kids laugh at you. Work hard and you'll learn. Avoid being put in "slow" classes because you don't know the language.

5. Busca ayuda de alguien que represente el programa bilingüe. Si tienes un problema, habla con tu consejera. La mayoría de los profesores son buenos y te ayudarán. Sé cortés y respetuoso con ellos. Debes llegar temprano. Saluda a tus profesores y amistades, y repasa tus tareas. Cuando suene la campana, sal de la clase calladamente y ve rapidamente a tu próxima clase. Obedece los reglamentos de la escuela. No seas una persona charlatana. No escribas en los pupitres o paredes. Tome orgullo en tu escuela y ciudad.

5. Find help from somebody who represents the bilingual program. If you have a problem, talk to your guidance counselor. Almost all the teachers are nice and will help you. Be polite and respectful to them. Get to school early, say hello to your teacher and friends, and look over your homework. When the bell rings, leave the room quietly and go quickly to be on time to your next class. Obey the rules. Don't be a "wise guy." Don't write on the desks or walls. Take pride in your school and city.

El que a buen árbol se arrima
buena sombra le cobija.

6. *Amistades.* Ten cuidado de la clase de amistades que escojes. Busca una persona que viva cerca de ti y hable tu propio lenguaje, pero que también hable inglés para que te explique cualquier problema que puedas tener con tu nuevo lenguaje. Lo peor que puedes hacer es estar siempre con personas que hablen solo español todo el tiempo, porque no vas a poder practicar lo que aprendes en tus clases. Trata de relacionarte con personas americanas para que te seas obligado a usar el inglés. No creas que todos los americanos son blancos y ricos. Trata de tener amistades y aprender acerca de las diferentes actividades en la escuela. Ingresa en algunas actividades y aprenderás más inglés y te sentirás parte de la escuela.

6. *Friends.* Be careful of the kinds of friends you choose. Look for someone who speaks your native language, lives near you and goes to the same school. Try to find someone who speaks Spanish and English and who can explain things to you and to whom you can explain any problem you may have. Choose friends who will help you with the language and will understand your problems. The worst thing you can do is to stay with only Spanish speakers all the time because you're not going to practice what you learn in class. Try to be with American people so you're forced to use English. Don't think all Americans are rich and/or white. Try to make friends and learn about the different activities in the school. Join some and you'll learn more English and feel a part of the school.

7. Debes de ver los programas americanos en la televisión, y también oir la radio en inglés. Trata de imitar su pronunciación. Practica la mejor pronunciación posible.

8. Entiende sobre las cuatro estaciones. Se pone muy frío en el invierno. Tienes que vestirte con ropa caliente. Evita enfermarte.

9. Ten cuidado de hablar con personas extrañas en la calle. Las ciudades grandes son muy diferentes a los pueblos pequeños. No vayas a ninguna parte con alguien que no conozcas, especialmente en un carro.

10. Tienes que tener interés en aprender, si no quieres aprender, no hay forma en que aprendas. Debes estudiar mucho porque si tu deseas algo no lo vas a encontrar en la calle. Tienes que trabajar fuertemente para obtenerlo, y lo obtendrás. "No hay almuerzos gratis alla fuera."

Buena suerte. Esperamos que hallamos hecho tu comienzo en este país más fácil. Bienvenidos a Passaic.

7. Watch American TV and listen to American announcers on radio. Try to imitate their pronunciation. Practice the best pronunciation possible.

8. Understand about the four seasons here. It can be very cold in winter. You have to have warm clothing. Avoid getting ill.

9. Be careful about talking to strangers away from school. The big city is very different from small villages. Don't go anywhere with someone you don't know, especially in a car.

10. You have to be interested in learning because if you don't want to learn, there is no way that you will. Study hard because if you want something, you are not going to find it on the street. You have to work hard for it and you will find it. "There is no free lunch out there."

Good luck. We hope we have made your beginnings here a little easier. Welcome to Passaic.

APPENDIX C

The Telephone
An aid to educators

The following is a partial listing of nationwide services that are available *free of charge* from the Bell Telephone System. To arrange for a program in your school or to obtain any of the materials listed below, call your local Bell Telephone Business Office. The number is listed in the front pages of your phone book. In some areas of the country, bilingual materials and services may also be available. (If your area is *not* serviced by the Bell Telephone System, your telephone company will still probably offer many of the same types of services and materials. Check with your local or regional office for information.)

I. *Visits, Tours, and Displays*

A. Visits to Telephone Offices:

Why not take your students on a tour of your local telephone central office building? The children will be fascinated to see the complex equipment and accounting facilities. Arrangements can also be made to see other telephone facilities such as Western Electric and AT&T Long Lines installations.

B. Special Displays:

Informative displays on the history of the telephone, current telephone service, phones for the handicapped, electronic switching, the laser, and other telephone-oriented subjects are available for school programs.

II. *Interesting Booklets*

Many informative, easy-to-read booklets on telephone topics are available, including one on telephone manners.

1. *Alexander Graham Bell*—True life story of the dreams, visions, and tireless work of the inventor of the telephone. It provides a concise biography of Mr. Bell, describing his early research and experiments in fields of speech and sound which ultimately led to the birth of the telephone. Mr. Bell's pioneering efforts in fields other than communications are also covered.

2. *Birth and Babyhood of the Telephone*—An informative booklet detailing the work of Thomas A. Watson, who, as Alexander Graham Bell's assistant, played a significant role in the development of the telephone.

3. *How the Telephone Works*—A simplified explanation of how the telephone works. The illustrations and text explain the many intricate parts of a telephone, as well as how a telephone call is placed, switched, and completed.

4. *Secretary and the Telephone*—The important role of today's secretary and how best to represent the boss.

5. *Telephone at Your Command*—An illustrated booklet explaining in detail the development of telephone switching equipment. It deals with the early problems of interconnecting telephones, crossbar switching equipment which is used in many of our central offices, and includes the newest electronic switching systems.

III. *Educational Aids*

A. Programs and Games

1. *Telezonia*—An instructional package for *elementary grades* designed to assist the teacher in presenting a complete program on good telephone usage and courtesy. It includes telephone sets, teacher's guide, student text, wall charts, and audiovisual presentations. A Spanish-language version also is available.

2. *Thank You, Please Call Again*—A training program utilizing the six-button telephone, designed to help students master telephone skills and courtesy in simulated business situations. It includes film strip, audio cassette, spirit masters, wall posters, and a teacher's guide.

3. *New City Telephone*—An educational simulation game designed to give students experience in group dynamics. They learn goal-setting, group decision-making, listening, note-taking, and some business and economic concepts. Teacher's manual, student manual and recorded cassettes are included.

4. *Career Education*—Various programs in skills development and career awareness. Programs encouraging minorities and women to enter the field of engineering are also available.

B. Special Education Programs

1. *The Magic of Speech*—A communications skills program to help correct articulation disorders. It includes a teacher's guide, student booklet, and wall posters, and utilizes the Teletrainer.

2. *Speaking Over Barriers*—A program to teach elementary-level educable and adult trainable mentally retarded people to use the telephone for social, business, and emergency purposes. It includes a teacher's guide, flash cards, and flip charts, and utilizes the Teletrainer.

IV. *Programs by Speakers*

Carefully selected programs, featuring audiovisuals, are available for your students. However, in most cases a minimum audience is requested.

	Level	*Title*
1.	*Secondary/Adult*	*Consumer Quiz*

An entertaining quiz program that increases the audience's awareness of laws and regulations protecting consumers. The speaker selects two teams from the audience and asks each questions on different areas of consumerism. Electronic score-keeping equipment helps simulate a TV quiz show atmosphere.

2.	*Elementary/ Secondary/Adult*	*Join In, Reach Out*

A moving color film illustrating how handicapped children and others are living fuller, happier lives through the use of devices developed by the Telephone Pioneers of America. A speaker introduces the film with a brief background about the Pioneers and their contributions to community service and demonstrates several of the devices.

3.	*Secondary/Adult*	*Pathways*

An interesting program showing how the nationwide telecommunications network is meeting the changing and growing communications needs of the American public. Features a 23-minute film with scenes in cities, remote villages, schools, hospitals, and offices.

4.	*Secondary/Adult*	*Silent World*

Oceanography and the story of the latest efforts to develop the many untapped resources of the ocean. Through sound tapes you hear some of the creatures that inhabit the so-called silent world. Color slides.

V. *Films*

16-mm sound films are available on a wide range of topics that may be of interest to your students. Be sure to book your request as far in advance as possible to avoid disappointment.

A. General

	Level	Title	Duration
1.	*Elementary/ Secondary/ Adult*	*About a Century*	28½ minutes

This film is a nostalgic reminiscence of the past 97 years. The story deals with the changing American scene from the peaceful days of farming and cattle raising to the age of electronics. The theme is light and sentimental, with appeal for young and old.

	Level	Title	Duration
2.	*Secondary/ Adult*	*All Kinds of People*	28 minutes

A look into the operation of Bell System Companies with emphasis on people and their dedication to service.

	Level	Title	Duration
3.	*Elementary/ Secondary/ Adult*	*Anything You Want to Be*	28 minutes

A fast-paced documentary on men and women in "non-traditional" jobs throughout business and industry, in schools, religious institutions, government, etc. Participants, including Bell System employees, were filmed in their work environment, describing their own experiences, feelings, and their perception of other employees' feelings toward them, at a wide variety of on-location sites.

	Level	Title	Duration
4.	*Elementary/ Secondary/ Adult*	*Baby-Sitter*	18 minutes

A dramatization of the proper techniques of babysitting. The story, as seen through the eyes of the baby, is lightly told by instructing without lecturing. Covers responsibilities of parents as well as baby-sitters.

	Level	Title	Duration
5.	*Elementary/ Secondary/ Adult*	*Beyond All Barriers*	28 minutes

The vital role communications plays in bringing people of the world together for better understanding.

	Level	Title	Duration
6.	*Elementary/ Secondary/ Adult*	*Connecting*	14 minutes

Shows telephone men and women as human beings—skilled craftspeople serving the public in a variety of ways and locations.

	Level	Title	Duration
7.	*Secondary/ Adult*	*Construction for Survival*	17½ minutes

Tells the story of the Bell System's efforts to protect cables and provide continuous service in the face of any natural or manmade disaster.

	Level	Title	Duration
8.	*Elementary/ Secondary/ Adult*	*Discovery*	28 minutes

This is a film about science. It relates understanding nature to curiosity, creativity, and communications, showing their importance to achievements in science. A point of view many scientists have about their work is described while pointing out the difference between science and technology.

	Level	Title	Duration
9.	*Secondary/ Adult*	*ESS—A Touch of Tomorrow*	12½ minutes

A behind-the-scenes look at the development of ESS (Electronic Switching Systems). Teamwork and technological skills of employees of the Bell System are shown through modern techniques in filmmaking.

10.	*Secondary/ Adult*	*Everyday Champions*	23 minutes

Handicapped Bell System employees tell their own stories. Through interviews, the film covers a wide range of topics related to employment, legislation, the hiring process, advancement opportunities, and special accommodations.

11.	*Elementary/ Secondary*	*Experiments*	7 minutes

Three children building a telephone system out of paper cups and string while others tour Bell Laboratories and learn about development of various means of transmission tell this story of experimentation and how it bears on researchers attempting to help people communicate with one another.

12.	*Elementary/ Secondary/ Adult*	*Generations*	32 minutes

A look at the generation gap with youngsters and adults talking about drugs, lifestyles, patriotism, and pollution.

13.	*Elementary/ Secondary/ Adult*	*Hello, I Need to Tell You Something*	20 minutes

Illustrates the difficulties of interpersonal communications while emphasizing our universal need to communicate. Stress is on the need for effective communication in all its broad aspects—including problems people have conversing with each other.

	Level	Title	Duration
14.	*Elementary/ Secondary/ Adult*	*How Did You Do That?*	7½ minutes

This film employs a dramatization to demonstrate the four Custom Calling Services and provides a general understanding of how they work. They are: "Call Waiting," "Call Forwarding," "Three-way Calling," and "Speed Calling." The approach is light and informative.

15.	*Secondary/ Adult*	*Incredible Machine*	15 minutes

This motion picture shows some of the almost fantastic ways Bell Laboratories' scientists are using computers in communications research. It contains sequences of computer generated movies, music, and speech.

16.	*Elementary/ Secondary/ Adult*	*It Couldn't Be Done*	55 minutes 2 reels

Engineering marvels people said "couldn't be done." Mt. Rushmore, the Panama Canal, the Hoover Dam, the Golden Gate Bridge, and more. They're all brought to life through animation, historical footage, and new film. Lee Marvin narrates with musical background by the Fifth Dimension.

17.	*Elementary/ Secondary/ Adult*	*It's All in a Day's Work*	14½ minutes

This service-oriented film depicts the Bell System's continuing commitment to equal opportunity, including scenes of male operators and service representatives and female plant personnel. It stresses the determination of Bell people to serve the public—sometimes under trying conditions.

	Level	Title	Duration
18.	*Elementary/ Secondary/ Adult*	*Sing a Sign*	28 minutes

This production features dance, mime, and poetry and is intended for everyone—both the deaf and the hearing audience. Its cast consists of young deaf and hearing singers, dancers, and actors. Performers include Rita Corey, star of the National Theater of the Deaf, and Susan Davidoff, who holds the title of Miss Deaf America.

	Level	Title	Duration
19.	*Secondary/ Adult*	*To Help Themselves*	12 minutes

Deals with the Bell System's efforts in the important area of designing, adapting, and providing telephone communications services for the physically handicapped, thereby enabling them to take their place in today's society.

	Level	Title	Duration
20.	*Secondary/ Adult*	*Before It's Too Late*	13½ minutes

Dick Van Dyke encourages the use of auto seat belts in this film based on an incident in which a seat belt saved his life.

	Level	Title	Duration
21.	*Elementary/ Secondary/ Adult*	*Fire*	13 minutes

Shows proper techniques for fighting electrical, gasoline, and paper fires, as well as how carelessness can cause them.

	Level	Title	Duration
22.	*Secondary/ Adult*	*Memento*	10 minutes

Without being gory or "preachy" this film provides a vivid insight into the problems of driver attitudes—a major cause of highway accidents in this country.

	Level	Title	Duration
23.	*Secondary/ Adult*	*The Party's Over*	9 minutes

Scenes of a party in progress are interwoven with glimpses of two young people preparing to go to a party. Close-ups emphasize the attention they give to their preparations and the inattention to their seat belts.

	Level	Title	Duration
24.	*Secondary/ Adult*	*Extra Step*	33 minutes

This film is directed at improving all communications—face-to-face and written, as well as on the telephone.

	Level	Title	Duration
25.	*Secondary/ Adult*	*How to Lose Your Best Customer—Without Really Trying*	25 minutes

Illustrates the problems that beset one small business with poor telephone habits. The situation is first shown "before" and then as it would have happened after analysis and corrective training.

APPENDIX D

Additional Housing Rights and Resources

Regardless of the type of community in which your students live, housing problems will still exist, although there are probably more to be found in urban and suburban areas. If you or your students have a housing question, call your local Housing and Urban Development (HUD) office. (For housing problems outside the United States, consult your local, regional, or national housing authority for assistance.) If they can't help you, they will refer you to someone who can. For problems that can't be resolved on the local level, contact:

Director
Federal Consumer Complaint Center
U.S. Office of Consumer Affairs
Department of Commerce
Washington, D.C. 20230

Be sure to tell your students (and their parents) that *any and all* housing problems should be promptly reported to their local HUD office. HUD is one of the few government agencies whose policies are developed on the basis of complaints. Our voices *do* count.

APPENDIX E

Consumer Education

"Caveat emptor" means you

Feeling ambitious? You might want to run off copies of this for your students and their families. It's the kind of information many native speakers of English aren't aware of. You might even want to make a project out of it involving your students supplying copies to the history or social studies teacher, or to a family friend, home economics class, and so on. In most cases, the publications listed are available in bulk to teachers.

1. To complain to or commend the *Federal Communications Commission (FCC)* about any aspect of television programming, including advertising, write to:

Consumer Assistance Office
Federal Communications
  Commission
Washington, D.C. 20554

Why not send for FCC's free newsletter, *Feedback,* which uses plain English to explain their proposals? You can have your students write to the above address to have their names put on the mailing list.

2. To participate in consumer training and regular regional meetings and/or discuss a drug or food-related problem, students can contact their local *Food and Drug Administration (FDA)* office. Look in the white pages under "U.S. Government." For a free subscription to FDA's newsletter, *Consumer Update,* write to:

Associate Commissioner of
  Consumer Affairs
Food and Drug Administration
5600 Fishers Lane
HF7 - Room 1685
Rockville, Maryland 20857

3. To participate in one of the *Department of Housing and Urban Development's* semiannual free consumer education programs in your state and/or to offer suggestions for appropriate topics for future public sessions, have your students call the local HUD office. It, too, is listed in the white pages under "U.S. Government."

4. To obtain the following free consumer publications, have any student who is interested print his or her name, address, and the stock number (if given) on a postcard and mail it to:

Consumer Information Center
Department CA
Pueblo, Colorado 81009

Publication	*Ordering Information*
Consumer Information Catalog	1981, 16 pp.
Consumer Resource Handbook	1980, 76 pp., #619J
Student Guide: Grants and Loans	1981, 16 pp., #535J

5. To contact their *Senator* or *Congressional Representative* about a matter relating to consumer affairs, or for any other special assistance that your students or their parents might need that they have *not* been able to resolve at the *local* level, have them write to him or her at either of the following addresses:

Name of Senator
U.S. Senate
Washington, D.C. 20510

Name of Congressional
Representative
U.S. House of Representatives
Washington, D.C. 20515

Representatives can be contacted through (202) 224-3121, the U.S. Capitol switchboard.

For assistance in resolving a consumer education problem outside the United States, contact your local, regional, or national consumer affairs office.

APPENDIX F

Writing Booklet Samples

SAMPLE BOOKLET I: Christmas Brings Memories

This book is dedicated to our families, our countries, and our friends, old and new.

PREFACE

What you are about to read comes from the hearts of students for whom English is a second language, and for whom the United States is a new home, at least the part of the United States called "The Mainland."

Christmas evokes memories of times past, and the students whose works you are sharing have written about something dear to them. We are neither professional writers nor professional typists, so we beg your indulgence. We hope you will enjoy our Christmas gift to you.

Mona Scheraga
and the Period Seven Class
Advanced ESL

December, 19 ____
Passaic High School
Passaic, New Jersey

"Dancing" by Juanita Colón[1]

Dominican Republic

Christmas to me means dancing, in my country and here. I just love dancing. When I'm dancing, I feel like in the sky, especially when I'm moving my waist. Well, dance is a very nice hobby because when you're sad and you hear a song, you feel a change. Your forget every single problem that you have but you have to know the kind of music. That goes with your feeling, because if the song is romantic and you are sad, you're not going to feel good. But if it is a happy song, oh my God, you feel so good.

[1]Only the names of the students have been changed. The words, sentiments, and syntax are exactly as they expressed them.

Cesar Diaz

Puebla, Mexico

I was born in Mexico, and I like my country very much, especially at Christmas-time. I like my country for a lot of things and one is because I was born there, and another is because I am an Indian, not a real Indian but I am. In my country, it is not cold at Christmas.

I like my state of Puebla, specially my town. The state of Puebla has a lot of beautiful things like the Cathedral of the city of Puebla. Cholula is near Puebla and there is the piramide (pyramid) more wide than the pyramids of Egypt. This pyramid is more wide not high. And the pyramid is beautiful on the inside. It has a cave and in the cave has how the Indians wrote before, and in other places are the Grutas De Cacahuamilpa, that are caves and those caves have a lot of beautiful things like little pictures; but those pictures are made by the water and the floor is too slippery. And I love my state of Puebla and my country, and here when somebody asks where I'm from, I say with pride, "I'm from Mexico." And I am one hundred percent Mexican. There's no place like Mexico at Christmas!

12/17/__

SAMPLE BOOKLET II: Our Lives

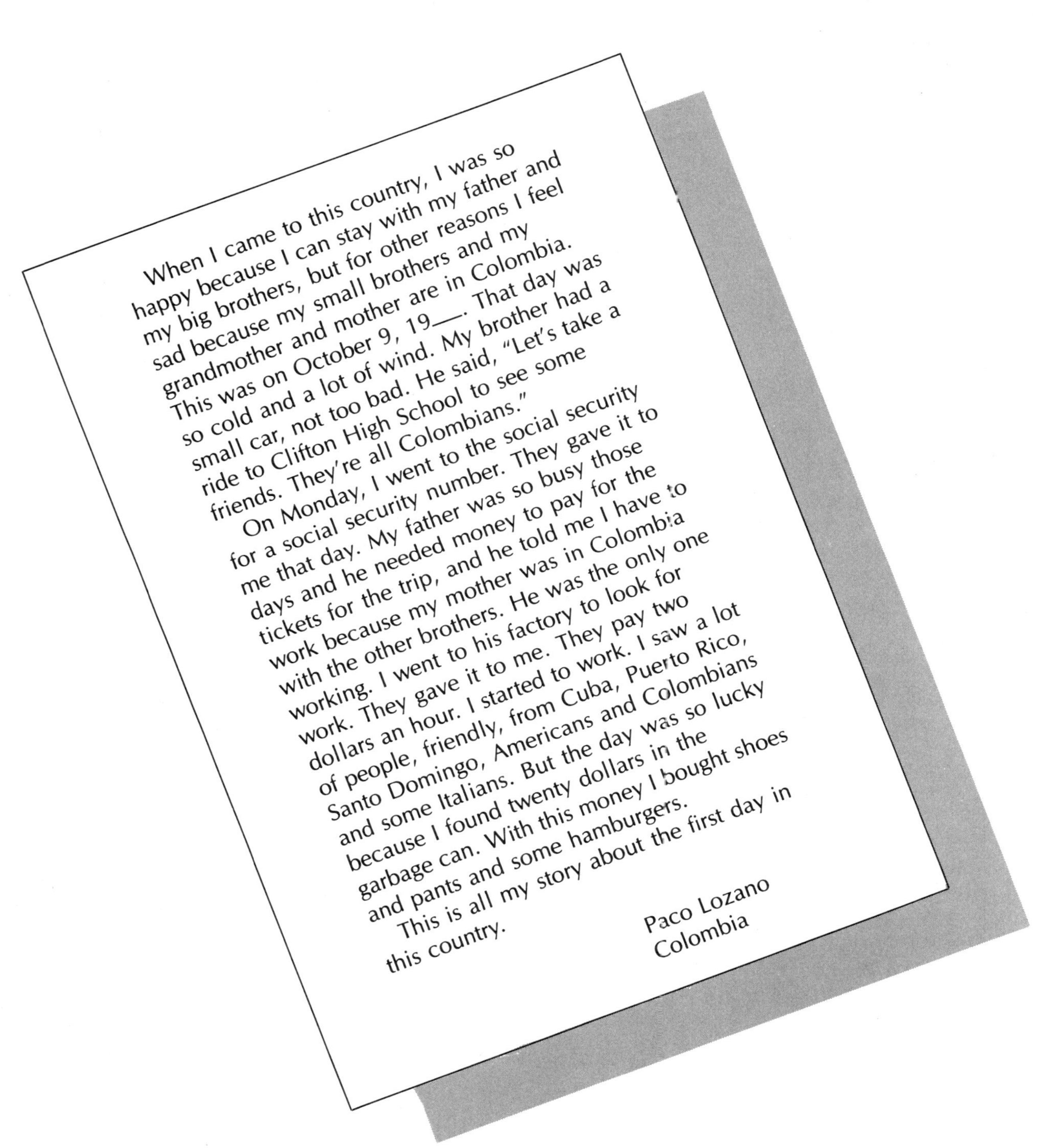

When I came to this country, I was so happy because I can stay with my father and my big brothers, but for other reasons I feel sad because my small brothers and my grandmother and mother are in Colombia. This was on October 9, 19___. That day was so cold and a lot of wind. My brother had a small car, not too bad. He said, "Let's take a ride to Clifton High School to see some friends. They're all Colombians."

On Monday, I went to the social security for a social security number. They gave it to me that day. My father was so busy those days and he needed money to pay for the tickets for the trip, and he told me I have to work because my mother was in Colombia with the other brothers. He was the only one working. I went to his factory to look for work. They gave it to me. They pay two dollars an hour. I started to work. I saw a lot of people, friendly, from Cuba, Puerto Rico, Santo Domingo, Americans and Colombians and some Italians. But the day was so lucky because I found twenty dollars in the garbage can. With this money I bought shoes and pants and some hamburgers.

This is all my story about the first day in this country.

Paco Lozano
Colombia

MY FIRST DAY IN SCHOOL

When I came to school I felt a little like a mouse in front of an elephant. I saw the people very strange. I didn't understand when they talk to me. My only response was yes for everything and when I went to New York, I became very disappointed because I was imagining New York a beautiful city and nice and clean streets. And I was imagining the American people very tall with blue eyes, and when I came here I saw that it was not the way I was thinking, and I was lost. For me, it was a very big school and too many people. I felt really all alone. A few weeks later I found a few friends so that was a little change for me.

Elba Rivera
Colombia

IN WINTER

I.

In winter we arrived
In winter we are. Don't you think
Winter is a beautiful season?
What else do I need to be aware
That winter is a beautiful season.

II.

Is it the white beautiful snow?
Is it that I need to see the sky
Which star could not shine because
Snow is coming to purify
the air?

Yes, winter is a beautiful season

Sergio Castellanos
Dominican
Republic

SAMPLE BOOKLET III: Something to Remember

When I came to this country, I felt very sad because I left my country and almost all my family. I went to school after fifteen days. When I went to school that first day, it was like when you go to school for the first time in your life.

I didn't know anybody. I was an ape. When I went to the homeroom, the teacher started to ask me things. I felt like running away from school and not go any more. My first weeks were very bad but I was lucky and I went to Spanish classes and then I started to make friends. I still miss my country and my family but now it is not like it was before. I have been here three years and I feel like this country is my country too.

Simón Puntos
Cuba

My name is Adel Jarkesy. I am from Jordan. I am Arab. I love my country and I love the United States too.

I came to the United States four months ago and I went to some cities in New Jersey and I went to the capital, Washington, D.C. I saw that city is very nice and very beautiful.

I have some trouble with the English language because in my country English is spoken differently and that is why I don't understand, and now I speak English some things very well.

Adel Jarkesy
Jordan

My country is one big island in the Mediterranean Sea on the other side of the world. My country's name is Cyprus and it's a Greek Island. The summers it was full of tourists in our towns and the tourists bring so much money with them. Everything was beautiful: our towns, our sea, the mountains, the old things and our manners and customs they were so good. But from 20 of July 1974 the war with the Turks started and all of the tourists left and the Turkish rule started. But the United Nations stopped them and the peace started coming, slow-slow in my country. But it was too late because too many innocent people lost their lives, about four thousand.

Now in my country everywhere you go you can see ruins of the war. But the Greek Cypriots they go to put out the Turks and we go to live alone like all of the other world, with peace. And we go to build up our hotels and houses and everything and the tourists are going to return and my country is going to be again lovely and rich.

This is my country like it was before the war and after the war. I love so much my country.

Demos Beys
Cypress

I have been here about five months. My great problem over here is that I haven't found any close friend to me, even at school, which is the best place for finding trustful and good friends. I don't know why. Maybe I am a new student or foreign or maybe I don't talk to someone. I'm usually afraid to talk, particularly with Americans. I can't conquer this feeling so I don't ask them anything. I have seen a lot of foreigners were laughed at by Americans when they make a mistake in talking and so on. I know the best way to learn English is to speak with someone else, but when there is no one, what is the result? In my home, if you are a good student, always the others come around you and are attracted to you and that is one of the best ways to choose a good friend, faithful and trustful, but here I am the best pupil in math and chem. class and when my classmates have some difficulty, they ask me about that, and after that, they forget everything about my favor. We have a proverb in Persian about these kinds of peoples; that is "when they are in trouble and have a problem they remember us, but then when they are happy, they forget us."

Parvis Maftoon
Iran

SAMPLE BOOKLET IV: Remembrance and Some Thoughts

The first time I came to this country, I was eight years old. I had heard too much of the United States and I was anxious to know all about it. When I came here, I felt happy. The truth is that I did not find it as I had imagined because I was thinking it was a peaceful country and not as it is, with a great quantity of bad people in the street. The first days I was so timid, but I came to school and could not speak because I had never seen so many things. All was strange for me. At last I saw that I was at home and that all were brothers. Now all feel together when we are sad or happy. Just now all goes fine. Beautiful.

Jorge Cesteño
Puerto Rico

My mother says that I have to study medicine or anything else but not go to the army. I've not decided what to study for but I think I'm going to study computer service. I explain to my mother to study this service it is necessary to go to the army. One night my brother asked me, "What are you doing tomorrow? What will be your future?" I didn't know what to tell him. "Why don't you study to be a business man?" I don't like this because I studied this class. I need to study Algebra. But he went away and there was no more discussion.

Mauricio Castro
Colombia

I am from Puerto Rico. I was born in a little town, Aguada. There I have many friends. When I was there I was very busy all day. Sometimes I went fishing. Other times I was riding a bicycle and many other things. When I had my vacation, I went to my grandmother's house and she is nice with me and she cares about me too much. I love her. It doesn't matter where I am.

Manny Pérez
Puerto Rico

The "Shmingus Dingus" means "besprinkle" or "water." That custom is a reminder from old magical intervention, assuring rain for crops. The ceremonial shape was very difficult, from discreet sprinkles to throwing the people into the river or pond. That custom started to disappear, and is adopted very rarely. Now people drip a perfume. The custom of sprinkling water is often used in the country. Today, on Shmingus Dingus Day in Poland boys throw water on girls and the day is for romance, like Valentine's Day here.

Stanley Kowalski
Poland

I was born in Poland - Krakow - When I was a small child my parents sent me to grammar school to learn basic education about the world and its minerals and natural resources. While studying in school, I learned many subjects. Meanwhile, I learned geography through which I found out about the ground and the things that happen in it. In my further studies I learned about the seven continents and their structure. At eight I dreamed that I will be in the United States because the older people described it to me that it is a very beautiful country and that is why I would want at least to see it. At the age of 14, I was told by my parents that we are going to the United States. I was very happy that my dream came true. Now I am 18 and I am in this country with my whole family. I am very happy and satisfied that I am learning a new language.

Mary Lukaszczyk
Poland

APPENDIX G

Criteria for Selecting Materials

Workbooks, dictionaries, textbooks, and other teaching aids

The question is not *"Why books?"* The answer to this would be as varied and valid as available textbooks themselves. The real question is *"Which books?"* To answer, you must first ask yourself:

1. what you expect the book(s) to achieve;

2. if any *one* book is sufficient for *all* your goals for the age/grade/proficiency level of ESL students you're teaching;

3. what your long-range and short-term goals for those students are;

4. how your own creative lesson plans can supplement the book(s) chosen and vice versa;

5. if your students would benefit more from several smaller, specialized texts or one basic text (age and number of students may be a consideration here);

6. how much money is available for texts and audiovisual aids.

Assuming there is a limited amount of funding (and when isn't there?), we consider certain kinds of materials essential for the ESL classroom:

1. *Pictures,* pictures, and more pictures are a must. You can save money by cutting colorful action shots, pictures of nouns and geographic and/or historic highlights from magazines. Have your students do so as part of a lesson plan (to see if they really do understand what a noun is, for example). You can also buy handsome commercial charts, often accompanied by textbooks or picture dictionaries or similar aids. Updated magnetic and flannel boards add variety and spark interest.

2. A *cassette player/recorder* should be part of an ESL teacher's tools. Again, depending on school finances, you may have to borrow one from your AV coordinator (assuming there is one and an AV department of some sort). Of course, if you don't request, you don't know. Ask for one of your own. You may be pleasantly surprised!

3. *Other aids,* such as record players, screens, film strip and/or slide projectors, overhead projectors, classroom computers, VCRs, add variety and spark to lessons. They can be borrowed as needed from the school resource center.

4. *Workbooks* can be a good secondary source of practice for your students if used properly. Ideally, students should be able to work in the workbooks themselves. Financially, this isn't always possible. Workbooks can be great for: practicing and reinforcing concepts learned and evaluating which concepts have truly been mastered. Our big complaint about workbooks is not the workbooks themselves. Many are intelligently and attractively prepared. They can be significantly helpful in assessing what learning has taken place and by whom. Unfortunately, the transference of skills learned doesn't always take place and we tend to wonder why. ESL students, not unlike native speakers of English, fail to apply to natural speech and writing what they seem to have learned as evidenced by their performance in workbooks. We suspect this is a universal problem that has to do with students not making the connection between *what* they are doing in the workbook and *why*.

As with all learning, the mastery of skills is only half the battle. Without the ability to apply these skills, the language learner is in no better position than the apprentice baker who has been trained to assemble the proper ingredients for a cake in the correct quantity, but does not yet have the confidence or experience to bake the cake on his or her own. Just as the ability to assemble ingredients, grease pans, light ovens, and set temperatures is merely a prelude to actually baking a cake, so the workbook/textbook user must understand that learning syntactic order, noun-verb agreement, placement, modifiers, and so forth are simply, or not so simply, necessary steps in the process of developing means for independent communication outside the workbook/textbook setting.

Again, in selecting workbooks for your students, you should:

a. decide what you want the workbooks to do;

b. examine as many different types as possible to see which best suit(s) your needs. (Examination copies are usually available from publishers on request.)

5. *Ditto masters* are another good secondary source. For those of us with permanently purple fingers and shirt sleeves, the convenience of commercially prepared ditto masters has some merit. They can be particularly useful as supplemental material, homework assignments, and instant lesson plans for substitutes not necessarily trained in ESL.

6. *Dictionaries* are an absolute necessity and must be tailored to the specific needs of ESL students:

a. *Monolingual dictionaries*—There should be one available for *every* student's use in class. Soft-cover may be less expensive but the most important aspect to consider is readability: Can your students, according to their age, grade, level of proficiency, get the information they need from the dictionaries you are considering for purchase?

1. Are the definitions understandable, appropriate, and when called for, varied?

2. Are there examples of how the word can be used in a sentence? If, for example, the word can be a noun and a verb, are there examples to illustrate both?

3. Are there illustrations and, if so, are they unbiased and can students easily make the association between picture and definition, or do they merely add to the confusion?

4. What other useful information does the dictionary offer the student besides a definition? (Is there an easy-to-use guide to pronunciation and syllabication, for example? Are synonyms and antonyms included, where appropriate? Is there an accompanying workbook?)

b. *Bilingual dictionaries*—There are bilingual picture dictionaries as well as a variety of soft-cover and hard-cover ones. Depending on the age, grade, and proficiency of your classes, you might want to have appropriate bilingual dictionaries available for those times when expediency dictates their use, or a misunderstanding can be clarified by referring to a bilingual source. For *beginners,* especially the more timid, at all age levels, bilingual dictionaries may be an essential "crutch" to make them more active and vocal participants in the learning process. We confess to keeping pocket dictionaries of all our students' native language backgrounds for those moments, rare as they may be, when communication begins with a smile and threatens to end with panic and fright because an essential word or thought is stuck somewhere mid-expression between brain and lips. While we understand that it may upset some of the purists among us, we don't feel it necessary to apologize for sacrificing purity for security. Our students come first!

It might be wise to assemble a group of dictionaries with the aforementioned in mind and, selecting several words your students might need to know, look them up. Think about some of those reasons other than obtaining definitions that might lead your students to use the dictionary. Consult the dictionaries you are considering for purchase and compare. Or, if you can bring them to class, have some of your students do so.

Another thought might be a trip to the school library where the same kind of "experiment" can be made. It will be clearer to you that dictionaries designed specifically for ESL students can be quite different from what we as native speakers have used and taken for granted all these years. Whatever you decide, examine a variety of what's out there and then always keep in mind *whom* you are teaching and what *their* dictionary needs are. (A debt of gratitude is owed to Della Summers Parish, Publisher, Longman House, England, for opening our eyes to the complexities involved in researching, writing, and publishing a dictionary. This, in turn, has taught us the incredible number of ways the sophisticated learner can make use of the dictionary.)

7. *Textbooks* and how you use them can be the difference between boredom and breakthrough. To parody a famous tune:

You must remember this
A book is just a book . . .

It's what you do with it that counts. But first you have to choose it. And if *you* are not the one to make the final selections, find out who is and volunteer your services as a professional interested in and knowledgeable about the quality of textbooks to be selected. If the "velvet glove approach" doesn't work, be persistent. Don't be afraid to demand. You and your students will be working with those books, possibly for several years. *Your input is essential.* Your demonstrated knowledge of what is available, from whom, the substance, quality, and format of different texts, will make it hard to legitimately exclude you from the selection process.

There are a variety of ways to investigate textbooks. Publishers are more than happy to send catalogues and/or publishers' representatives to you and your school district. Examination copies of texts are usually available free for thirty days. TESOL[1] and NABE[2] affiliate meetings and international conventions provide incredible displays of books and audiovisual materials designed specifically for an increasing ESL market. You and your ESL colleagues can easily orga-

[1]TESOL is the acronym for the International Association of Teachers of English to Speakers of Other Languages. (Washington, D.C., U.S.A.)
[2]NABE is the acronym for the National Association of Bilingual Educators. (Washington, D.C., U.S.A.)

nize your own book fair. We did. You, too, can be overwhelmed by the response from publishers, big and small. We need each other; we all need the students; and the students need books, the best books possible.

Things to Keep in Mind Before Ordering the Books

1. What is the general age/grade level you are teaching?

2. What is the general language proficiency level(s) of your students? (Are they adults who are functionally illiterate in their own language, teenagers who are preparing for college or the world of work, or perhaps third-graders just learning to read English?)

3. What are the reading levels of the texts?[3]

4. What materials and resources are available to you (your own materials, realia, previously enumerated audiovisual aids)?

5. Why do you want a text or textbooks? What are the purpose(s) you expect the text(s) to satisfy? (There is a growing number of ESL in the Content Area and English for Special Purposes materials to choose from today.)

6. Would your students benefit more from one text which covers all language skills, or would several smaller texts, each devoted to a specific skill or subskill, be more appropriate and/or more valuable psychologically and practically?

7. How much money is available for texts and how many of a particular set of books are needed?

a. Can the students take them home?

b. Can you order extras to ensure against shortages when one or more students inevitably lose a book?

c. If you're teaching more than one class of beginners, intermediate, or advanced, can you order sufficient textbooks so that your lesson plans can be, at best, vaguely similar?

8. Is this the latest/revised edition of the text, or will a new, updated edition be out a year or less after you've made your purchase? Caveat emptor: check with the publisher(s).

Kenneth Chastain points out that ". . . the acid test of any materials is the compatibility between these materials and the personality and teaching practices of the teacher." (Kenneth Chastain, *Developing Second-Language Skills: Theory to Practice,* Chicago: Rand McNally College Publishing Company, 1971, 524.) When examining texts, a teacher may feel almost instinctively that a particular format will or will not fit his or her needs. For those books that will or might, closer examination is required. The price, size, and durability of a text are not to be minimized; nor is the quantity and quality of the illustrations and/or photographs. There should be an awareness of the appropriateness of the illustrations and photographs (and any other pictorial material) and close, close scrutiny to be sure they are free of cultural, racial, sexual, and age bias. (See Jean D'Arcy Maculaitis, "Biased Language: The Urge to Purge," unpublished keynote address, Ninth Annual ESL Conference/In-Service, University of Manitoba, Winnipeg, Manitoba, Canada, February 1981 [available in ERIC] and other similar sources.)

The text itself should be attractively laid out, nonthreatening to a new language learner, and logically and linguistically sequential in complexity. It is exceedingly important to remember that while *vocabulary* must be appropriate to *proficiency* level, the *context* in which the vocabulary is used should be appropriate to the interests of the

[3]For example, you might wish to use the following: Edward B. Fry, *Fry Readability Scale,* Providence, Rhode Island: Jamestown Publishers, 1978.

age group you are working with. And above all, the vocabulary should be "real." "Although it is the most important, 'real' language is the phase of language teaching most often neglected." (Chastain, 527.) The word *jump,* for example, can be demonstrated in a primer with Alexis and Daniel jumping rope; a secondary ESL text might picture Theresa and David jumping hurdles, and in the adult text, there might be a paragraph which includes jumping batteries.

If you are "addicted" to one type of teaching style/technique, be it audiolingual, counseling learning, notional-functional, total physical response, the natural approach, or have an eclectic style, you will want to examine various texts to see which you *and* your students will be most comfortable with.

Besides appropriate vocabulary, subject matter and illustrations, you might want to examine the texts for:

1. natural language;

2. oral and/or written exercises;

3. practice drills;

4. glosssary;

5. role-playing opportunities;

6. sequential development of listening, speaking, reading, writing skills; and

7. cultural accuracy.

Should no one text satisfy *all* your needs, as has been our experience, begin by ordering those that satisfy the greatest number of them first. Continue to examine, evaluate, and order other texts as you can, always keeping in mind not only what is needed but for *whom* they are needed.

Also to bear in mind are the credentials of the author(s). It is relatively easy to ascertain academic credentials, professional backgrounds, years of actual ESL classroom experience, and *active* involvement in the discipline of English as a second language. *Don't just check out the book; check out the author(s)!*

References

The following code is used to indicate the appropriate level for each entry:
E = appropriate for elementary school students
S = appropriate for secondary school students
A = appropriate for adult education students

I. Articles

Bimes, Beverly J. "Total School Writing: A Working Approach to Writing Problems" in *Today's Education,* Washington, D.C.: National Education Association, April–May 1981, 32G–33G. (E/S/A)

Cardenas, José A. "The Role of Native-Language Instruction in Bilingual Education" in *Kappan,* Bloomington, Indiana: Phi Delta Kappa, Vol. 67, No. 5, January 1986, 359–363. (E/S)

Epstein, Jennifer L. "Teaching Vocational Library Skills To Refugees: How Do You Apply for a Job When You Have Never Held a Pencil?" in ERIC/CLL News Bulletin, Washington, D.C.: ERIC, Vol. 9, No. 1, September 1985, 5–8. (A)

Esaki, Alice, and Miriam Lykke. "Driver Education for LEP Students" in *TESOL Secondary School Interest Section Newsletter,* Washington, D.C.: Vol. 8, No. 3, August 1986, 6–8. (S)

Gersten, Russell, and Douglas Carnine. "Direct Instruction in Reading Comprehension" in *Educational Leadership,* Alexandria, Virginia: Association for Supervision and Curriculum Development, Vol. 43, No. 7, April 1986, 70–77. (S/A)

Haney, Walt. "Making Testing More Educational" in *Educational Leadership,* Alexandria, Virginia: Association for Supervision and Curriculum Development, Vol. 43, No. 7, October 1985, 4–13. (E/S/A)

Hull, Glynda, and David Bartholomae. "Teaching Writing as Learning and Process" in *Educational Leadership,* Alexandria, Virginia: Association for Supervision and Curriculum Development, Vol. 43, No. 7, April 1986, 44–53. (S/A)

Lesgold, Alan M. "Preparing Children for a Computer-Rich World" in *Educational Leadership,* Alexandria, Virginia: Association for Supervision and Curriculum Development, Vol. 43, No. 6, March 1986, 7–11. (E/S)

McBride, James R. "Computerized Adaptive Testing" in *Educational Leadership,* Alexandria, Virginia: Association for Supervision and Curriculum Development, Vol. 43, No. 7, October 1986, 25–28. (S/A)

McGuire, Willard. "Teacher Suggestions on Parent Involvement" in *Today's Education,* Washington, D.C.: National Education Association, April–May 1981, 9. (E/S/A)

Martin, John Henry. "Developing More Powerful Educational Software" in *Educational Leadership,* Alexandria, Virginia: Association for Supervision and Curriculum Development, Vol. 43, No. 6, March 1986, 32–34. (E/S)

Morley, Joan. "Listening Comprehension: Student-Controlled Modules for Self-Access Self-Study" in *TESOL Newsletter,* Washington, D.C.: TESOL, Vol. XIX, No. 6, December 1985, 1, 32–34. (S/A)

Murphey, Tim. "Teaching for Peak Relevance Using International Pop Music" in *TESOL Newsletter,* Washington, D.C.: TESOL, Vol. XIX, Vol. 6, December 1985, 13. (S/A)

Neubert, Gloria A., and Sally J. McNelis. "Improving Writing in the Disciplines" in *Educational Leadership,* Alexandria, Virginia: Association for Supervision and Curriculum Development, Vol. 43, No. 7, April 1986, 54–58. (S/A)

Pillsbury, Maurice. "Organized Writing Will Get You Your Tenure, Señor" unpublished essay, January 1981. (E/S)

Rich, Dorothy. "Building Good Home-School Relationships" in *Today's Education,* Washington, D.C.: National Education Association, February–March 1981, 68GE–69GE. (E/S)

Scheraga, Mona. "ESL with Advanced High School Students" in *TESOL Quarterly,* Washington, D.C.: TESOL, Vol. 14, No. 1, March 1980, 41–57. (S)

Taylor, Wilson, L. "Cloze Procedure: New Look for Measuring Readability" in *Journalism Quarterly,* XXX, 1953, 415–433. (E/S/A)

Valdez, Gilbert. "Realizing the Potential of Educational Technology" in *Educational Leadership,* Alexandria, Virginia: Association for Supervision and Curriculum Development, Vol. 43, No. 6, March 1986. 4–6. (E/S)

II. Games

Ahl, David H., ed. *Basic Computer Games.* (Microcomputer Bulletin), New York, New York: Workman Publishing, 1978. (E/S/A)

Benson, Bryan, and Lydia Stack. *Word Ways Cubes,* San Francisco, California: The Alemany Press, 1979. (E/S/A)

____________________. *Word Ways Gameboards,* San Francisco, California: The Alemany Press, 1979. (E/S/A)

____________________. *Word Ways Game Cards for Oral Development,* San Francisco, California: The Alemany Press, 1981. (E/S/A)

Chamberlin, Anthony, and Jack Stenberg. *Play and Practice!* Lincolnwood, Illinois: National Textbook Company, 1979. (E/S/A)

Lee, W. R. *Language Teaching Games and Contests.* New York: Oxford University Press, 1979. (E/S/A)

Liebowitz, Dorothy Gabel. *Basic Vocabulary Builder.* Lincolnwood, Illinois: National Textbook Company, 1980 (E/S/A)

McCallum, George P. *101 Word Games for Students of English as a Second or Foreign Language.* New York: Oxford University Press, 1980. (E/S/A)

Raudsepp, Eugene. *More Creative Growth Games.* New York: The Putnam Publishing Group, 1980. (S/A)

____________________. *How Creative Are You?* New York: The Putnam Publishing Group, 1981. (S/A)

Raudsepp, Eugene, and George Hough, Jr. *Creative Growth Games.* New York, New York: The Putnam Publishing Group, 1977. (S/A)

Schinke-Llano, Linda. *Vocabulary Games for English Language Learners.* Lincolnwood, Illinois: National Textbook Company, 1980. (E/S/A)

III. Handbooks

Amster, Beverly, and Jean D'Arcy Maculaitis. *The Creative ESL Secondary School Teacher: A Practical Handbook of Inexpensive Materials and Successful Techniques,* unpublished paper, San Francisco, California: 1980 TESOL Convention. (S/A)

Asher, James J. *Learning Another Language Through Actions: The Complete Teacher's Guidebook.* San Francisco, California: The Alemany Press, 1977. (E/S/A)

Bragstad, Bernice Jensen, and Sharyn Mueller Stumpf. *A Guidebook for Teaching: Study Skills and Motivation.* Boston, Massachusetts: Allyn and Bacon, Inc., 1982. (E/S/A)

Cleveland, Bernard F. *Master Teaching Techniques: Neuro-Linguistic Programming.* Stone Mountain, Georgia: The Connecting Link Press, 1986. (E/S/A)

Devine, Thomas G. *Teaching Study Skills: A Guide for Teachers.* Boston, Massachusetts: Allyn and Bacon, Inc., 1981. (E/S/A)

Hopkins, Lee Bennett, and Annette Frank Shapiro. *Creative Activities for the Gifted Child*. Belmont, California: Fearon Publishers, 1969. (E/S)

Junior Achievement. *Project Business*. Stanford, Connecticut: Junior Achievement, 1985. (E/S)

Nassif, Janet Zhun. *Handbook of Health Careers: A Guide to Employment Opportunities*. Washington, D.C.: Association for Educational Communications and Technology, 1981. (E/S/A)

Olsen, Judy E. Winn-Bell. *Communication Starters and Other Activities for the ESL Classroom*. San Francisco, California: The Alemany Press, 1977. (E/S/A)

Platts, Mary E. *Anchor: A Handbook of Vocabulary Discovery Techniques for the Classroom Teacher*. Stevensville, Michigan: Educational Service, Inc., 1970. (E)

____________________. *Launch: A Handbook of Early Learning Techniques for the Preschool and Kindergarten Teacher*. Stevensville, Michigan: Educational Service, Inc., 1972. (E)

Pusch, Margaret D., ed. *Multicultural Education: A Cross-Cultural Training Approach*. Yarmouth, Maine: Intercultural Press, Inc., 1979. (E/S/A)

Riverol, Armando. *ESL Action Reporter*. Hayward, California: The Alemany Press, 1983. (S/A)

Simon, Sidney, B., Leland W. Howe, and Howard Kirchenbaum. *Values Clarification: A Handbook of Practical Strategies for Teachers and Students*. New York: A and W Publishers, 1978. (E/S/A)

Smith, Samuel. *Best Methods of Study*. New York: Barnes & Noble Books, 1970. (E/S/A)

Spencer, Zane A. *Flair: A Handbook of Creative Writing Techniques for the Elementary School Teacher*. Stevensville, Michigan: Educational Service, Inc., 1972. (E)

Tschudin, Ruth Anne. *Educator's Deskbook of Ideas and Activities from Award-Winning Teachers*. West Nyack, New York: Parker Publishing Company, Inc., 1980, 36–49. (E/S)

Wellman, Laurie, et al. *English for Living Series*. Albany, New York: The State Education Department, 1979. (S/A)

IV. Reference Books or Sources

Allen, Virginia French. *Techniques in Teaching Vocabulary*. New York: Oxford University Press, 1983. (E/S/A)

Bandler, Richard. *Using Your Brain—for a Change: Neuro-Linguistic Programming*. Moab, Utah: Real People Press, 1985. (E/S/A)

Bandler, Richard, and John Grinder. *Frogs into Princes: Neuro-Linguistic Programming*. Moab, Utah: Real People Press, 1979. (E/S/A)

____________________. *Reframing: Neuro-Linguistic Programming and the Transformation of Meaning*. Moab, Utah: Real People Press, 1982. (E/S/A)

____________________. *The Structure of Magic: A Book About Language and Theory*. Palo Alto, California: Science and Behavior Books, Inc., 1975. (E/S/A)

Bolinger, Dwight, and Donald A. Sears. *Aspects of Language*. New York: Harcourt Brace Jovanovich, Inc., 1981. (E/S/A)

Bragstad, Bernice Jensen, and Sharyn Mueller Stumpf. *A Guidebook For Teaching Study Skills and Motivation*. Boston, Massachusetts: Allyn and Bacon, Inc., 1982. (E/S/A)

Bureau of Labor Statistics, U.S. Department of Labor. *BLS Job Pamphlets*. New York: U.S. Department of Labor, n.d. (S/A)

Buzan, Tony. *Use Both Sides of the Brain*. New York: E. P. Dutton, 1985. (E/S/A)

Carroll, Brendan J. *Testing Communicative Performance: An Interim Study*. New York: Pergamon Press, 1980. (E/S/A)

Chaille, David. *Teacher Survival Tips*. Beverly Hills, California: Easy Aids, Inc., 1978. (E/S/A)

Chamberlin, Anthony, and Kurt Stenberg. *Play and Practice!* Lincolnwood, Illinois: National Textbook Company, 1979. (E/S/A)

Chastain, Kenneth. *Developing Second Language Skills: Theory to Practice*. Chicago: Rand McNally College Publishing, 1976. (E/S/A)

Copperman, Paul. *Taking Book to Heart: How to Develop a Love of Reading in Your Child*. Reading, Massachusetts: The Addison-Wesley Publishing Company, Inc., 1986. (E)

Cullum, Albert. *The Geranium on the Window Sill Just Died but Teacher You Went Right On*. Belgium: Harlin Quist, Inc., 1971. (E/S)

Devine, Thomas G. *Teaching Study Skills: A Guide for Teachers*. Boston, Massachusetts: Allyn and Bacon, Inc., 1981. (E/S/A)

Dilts, Robert. *Applications of Neuro-Linguistic Programming*. Cupertino, California: Meta Publishers, 1983. (E/S/A)

Dilts, Robert, John Grinder, Richard Bandler and Judith DeLozier. *Neuro-Linguistic Programming: The Study of the Structure of Subjective Experience, Vol. 1*. Cupertino, California: Meta Publications, 1980. (E/S/A)

Fantini, Alvino E. *Language Acquisition of a Bilingual Child: A Sociolinguistic Perspective*. Brattleboro, Vermont: The Experiment Press, 1976. (E)

Federal Register. *Annual Occupational Outlook Handbook*. Washington, D.C.: United States Department of Labor, Bureau of Labor Statistics, 1990–1981. (S/A)

Finegan, Edward. *Attitudes Toward English Usage: The History of a War of Words*. New York: Teacher's College Press, 1980. (S/A)

Finocchiaro, Mary, and Sydney Sako. *Foreign Language Testing: A Practical Approach*. New York, New York: Regents Publishing Company, Inc., 1983. (E/S/A)

Flanagan, John C., William H. Shanner and Robert F. Mager. *Language Arts: Behavioral Objectives, Primary, Intermediate, and Secondary*. Palo Alto, California: Westinghouse Learning Press, 1971. (E/S)

Friedenberg, Joan E., and Curtis H. Bradley. *Finding a Job in The United States*. Passport Books, a division of NTC Publishing Group, 1986. (S/A)

Fry, Edward B. *Fry Readability Scale*. Providence, Rhode Island: Jamestown Publishers, 1978. (E/S/A)

Fry, Edward B., Jacqueline K. Polk and Dona Fountoukidis. *The Reading Teacher's Book of Lists*. Englewood Cliffs, New Jersey: Prentice-Hall, Inc., 1984. (E/S/A)

Grant, Gloria, ed. *In Praise of Diversity: Multicultural Classroom Applications*. Omaha, Nebraska: The University of Nebraska, Teacher Corps, Center for Urban Education, 1977. (E/S/A)

Greer, Colin. *The Great School Legend*. New York: Basic Books, Inc., 1972. (E/S)

Gordon, David. *Therapeutic Metaphors: Helping Others Through the Looking Glass*. Cupertino, California: Meta Publications, 1978. (E/S/A)

Gysbers, Norman C., and Associates. *Designing Careers: Counseling to Enhance Education, Work, and Leisure*. San Francisco, California: Jossey-Bass Publications, 1984. (S/A)

Hall, Edward T. *The Silent Language*. New York: Anchor Press, 1973. (E/S/A)

Hall, Janice K. *Evaluating and Improving Written Expression: A Practical Guide for Teachers*. Boston, Massachusetts: Allyn and Bacon, Inc., 1981. (E/S/A)

Hall, Nancy A. *Rescue: A Handbook of Remedial Reading Techniques for the Classroom Teacher*. Stevensville, Michigan: Educational Service, Inc., 1969. (E/S/A)

Harragan, Betty Lehan. *Games Mother Never Taught You: Corporate Gamesmanship for Women*. New York: Warner Books, Inc., 1978. (S/A)

Harvard Educational Review. *Challenging the Myths: The Schools, The Blacks, and the Poor.* Cambridge, Massachusetts: Harvard Educational Review, 1979. (E/S/A)

Hymes, Dell. *Language in Culture and Society: A Reader in Linguistics and Anthropology.* New York: Harper and Row Publishers, 1964. (E/S/A)

Jacobson, Sid. *Meta-Cation: Prescriptions for Some Ailing Educational Processes.* Cupertino, California: Meta Publications, 1983. (E/S/A)

Johnson, David W., and Roger T. Johnson. *Learning Together and Alone.* Englewood Cliffs, New Jersey: Prentice-Hall, Inc., 1975.

Karler, Clarence J., Paul Violos, and Joel Spring. *Roots of Crises: American Education in the Twentieth Century.* Rand McNally College Publishing Company, 1973. (E/S/A)

Lafayette, Robert C., ed. *The Cultural Revolution in Foreign Language Teaching.* Lincolnwood, Illinois: National Textbook Company, 1975. (E/S/A)

Lamatino, Robyn. *Twenty Trades to Read About: Spanish/English.* Trenton, New Jersey: New Jersey State Department of Education, Division of Vocational Education and Career Preparation, 1978. (S/A)

Lenox, James P. *Buscando un Empleo.* Trenton, New Jersey: State of New Jersey Department of Education, Division of Vocational Education and Career Preparation, 1979. (S/A)

Lewis, E. Glyn. *The Teaching of English as a Foreign Language in Ten Countries.* New York: Halsted Press Book, 1975. (A)

Maculaitis, Jean D'Arcy. "Biased Language: The Urge to Purge," unpublished keynote address, Ninth Annual ESL Conference/In-Service, University of Manitoba, Winnipeg, Manitoba, Canada, February 1981. (E/S/A)

Madsen, Harold S. *Techniques in Testing.* New York: Oxford University Press, 1983. (E/S/A)

Mager, Robert F., and Kenneth M. Beach, Jr. *Developing Vocational Instruction.* Palo Alto, California: Fearon Publishers, 1967. (S/A)

Marsh, Louise. *Rhyme and Reason: A Reference Handbook of Vowel Sounds and Spelling in American English.* San Francisco, California: The Alemany Press, 1979. (E/S/A)

Meade, James G. *The Rights of Parents and the Responsibilities of Schools.* Cambridge, Massachusetts: Educators Publishing Service, 1978. (E/A)

Morrison, Joan, and Charlotte Fox Zubusky. *American Mosaic: The Immigrant Experience in the Words of Those Who Lived It.* New York: E. P. Dutton, 1980. (E/S.A)

Nilsen, Alleen Pace, Haig Bosmagian, H. Lee Gershuny, and Julia P. Stanley. *Sexism and Language.* Urbana, Illinois: National Council of Teachers of English, 1977. (E/S/A)

Omaggio, Alice C. *Proficiency-Oriented Classroom Testing.* Washington, D.C.: The Center for Applied Linguistics, 1983. (E/S/A)

Parnwell, E. C. *Oxford Picture Dictionary of American English.* New York: Oxford University Press, 1978. (E)

Paulston, Christina Pratt. *What Research Says to the Teacher: English as a Second Language.* Washington, D.C.: National Education Association, 1980. (E/S/A)

Procter, Paul, ed. *Longman Dictionary of Contemporary English.* London, England: Longman Group Limited, 1978. (S/A)

Rosenthal, Marilyn S., and Daniel B. Freeman. *Longman Photo Dictionary.* New York: Longman Inc., 1986. (S/A)

Rubin, Joan, and Irene Thompson. *How to Be a More Successful Language Learner.* Boston, Massachusetts: Heinle & Heinle Publishers, Inc., 1982. (S/A)

Ruddell, Robert B. *Reading-Language Instruction: Innovative Practices.* Englewood Cliffs, New Jersey: Prentice-Hall, Inc., 1974. (E/S/A)

Scarcella, Robin C., and Stephen D. Krashen, eds. *Research in Second Language Acquisition: Selected Papers of the Los Angeles Second Language Acquisition Forum.* Rowley, Massachusetts: Newbury House Publishers, Inc., 1980. (E/S/A)

Scott, Foresman and Company. *Mi Diccionario Ilustrado—My Dictionary.* Glenview, Illinois: Scott, Foresman and Company, 1971. (E)

Seelye, Ned H. *Teaching Culture: Strategies for Foreign Language Educators.* Lincolnwood, Illinois: National Textbook Company, 1975. (E/S/A)

Shuman, R. Baird. *Questions English Teachers Ask.* Rochelle Park, New Jersey: Hayden Book Company, Inc., 1977. (E/S/A)

Spears, Richard A. *NTC's American Idioms Dictionary.* Lincolnwood, IL: National Textbook Company, 1987. (S/A)

Spolsky, Bernard, ed. *The Language Education of Minority Children.* Rowley, Massachusetts: Newbury House Publishers, Inc., 1972. (E/S)

Steensma, Connie. *Speaking With Confidence: How to Take the Worries Out of Business Presentations.* New York: Business Week, 1985. (S/A)

The Center for Applied Linguistics. *From the Classroom to the Workplace: Teaching ESL to Adults.* Washington, D.C.: The Center for Applied Linguistics, 1983. (A)

Turkel, Judi Kesselman, and Franklynn Peterson. *Test-Taking Strategies: How to Raise Your Scores on ALL Types of Tests.* Chicago, Illinois: Contemporary Books, Inc., 1981. (S/A)

Van Nagel, C., Robert Siudzinski, Edward J. Reese, and MaryAnn Reese. *Megateaching and Learning: Neuro-Linguistic Programming Applied to Education, Vol. 1.* Indian Rock Beach, Florida: Southern Institute Press, Inc., 1985., (E/S/A)

Wiederholt, J. Lee, Donald D. Hammill, and Virginia Brown. *The Resource Teacher: A Guide to Effective Practice.* Boston: Allyn and Bacon, Inc., 1978. (E/S)

Williams, Linda Verlee. *Teaching for the Two-Sided Mind: A Guide to Right Brain/Left Brain Education.* New York: Simon & Schuster, Inc., 1983.

Yeager, Joseph. *Thinking About Thinking With NLP.* Cupertino, California: Meta Publications, 1985. (S/A)

V. Textbooks

Azar, Betty Schrampfer. *Understanding and Using English Grammar.* Englewood Cliffs, New Jersey: Prentice-Hall, Inc., 1981. (S/A)

Boggs, Ralph S., and Robert J. Dixon. *English Step by Step with Pictures.* New York: Regents Publishing Company, Inc., 1980. (E/S/A)

Church, Nancy, and Anne Moss. *How to Survive in the U.S.A.: English for Travelers and Newcomers.* New York: Cambridge University Press, 1986. (S/A)

Cornelius, Edwin T. *Interview.* New York: Longman, Inc., 1981. (S/A)

De Garcia, Karen Batchelor, and Randi Slaughter. *In Plain English: An Integrated Skills Approach.* Reading, Massachusetts: Addison-Wesley Publishing Company, Inc., 1986. (A)

________________. *More Plain English: An Integrated Skills Approach.* Reading, Massachusetts: Addison-Wesley Publishing Company, Inc., 1986. (A)

Dresner, Joanne, Kenneth Beck, Clare Morgano, and Luise Custer. *It's Up to You: Language Skills and Strategies for Getting a Job.* New York: Longman, Inc., 1980. (S/A)

Ekwall, Elden E. *Locating and Correcting Reading Difficulties.* Columbus, Ohio: Charles E. Merrill Publishing Company, 1970. (E/S/A)

Gonshack, Sol. *Little Stories for Big People.* New York: Regents Publishing Company, Inc., 1976. (S/A)

Hill, L. A. *Elementary Anecdotes in American English.* New York: Oxford University Press, 1980. (S/A)

Jones, Leo, and C. Von Baeyer. *Functions of American English: Communication Activities for the Classroom.* New York: Cambridge University Press, 1986. (S/A)

Kimbrough, Victoria, Donn Byrne, and Michael Palmer. *Odyssey: A Communicative Course in English, Vol. 1–6.* New York: Longman, Inc., 1984. (S)

Krulik, David, and Barbara Zaffran. *Everyday English as a Second Language, Vol. 1–4.* Lincolnwood, Illinois: National Textbook Company, 1981. (S/A)

Light, Richard. *Teaching English as a Second Language: Perspectives and Practices, Vol. 1–6.* Albany, New York: The University of the State of New York, 1978. (E/S/A)

Live, Anna Harris, and Suzanne Harris Sandowsky. *American Mosaic: Intermediate–Advanced ESL Reader.* Englewood Cliffs, New Jersey: Prentice-Hall, Inc., 1980. (S/A)

McKay, Sandra, and Lisa Rosenthal. *Writing for a Special Purpose.* Englewood Cliffs, New Jersey: Prentice-Hall, Inc., 1980. (S/A)

McPartland, Pamela. *American Idioms: Take It Easy.* Englewood Cliffs, New Jersey: Prentice-Hall, Inc., 1981. (E/S/A)

Maggs, Margaret Martin. *English Across the Curriculum, Vol. 1–3.* Lincolnwood, Illinois: National Textbook Company, 1983. (S)

———————. *Building Vocabulary, Vol. A, B, C.* Lincolnwood, Illinois: National Textbook Company, 1981. (S/A)

Mellgren, Lars, and Michael Walker. *Yes! English for Children.* Reading, Massachusetts: Addison-Wesley, 1977. (E/S)

Mitchell, Joyce Slayton. *See Me More Clearly: Career and Life Planning for Teens with Physical Disabilities.* New York: Harcourt Brace Jovanovich, 1981. (S/A)

Molinsky, Steven J., and Bill Bliss. *Side by Side: English Grammar Through Guided Conversations.* Englewood Cliffs, New Jersey: Prentice-Hall, Inc., 1980. (S/A)

Raimes, Ann. *Exploring Through Writing: A Process Approach to ESL Composition.* New York: St. Martin's Press, 1986. (S/A)

Richards, Jack C., ed. *Error Analysis: Perspectives on Second Language Acquisition.* London: Longman Group Limited, 1974. (E/S/A)

Schoenberg, Irene E. *Talk About Trivia: 1001 Questions.* New York: Longman Inc., 1986. (A)

Simms, Jean, and Patricia Wilcox Peterson. *Better Listening Skills.* Englewood Cliffs, New Jersey: Prentice-Hall, Inc., 1981. (S/A)

Smith, Charlene W. *The Listening Activity Book: Teaching Literal, Evaluative, and Critical Listening in the Elementary School.* Belmont, California, 1975. (E)

Tillett, Bruce, and Mary Newton Bruder. *Speaking Naturally: Communication Skills in American English.* New York: Cambridge University Press, 1986. (S/A)

Van Dien, Tran, and Winabelle Gritter. *Folk Tales for Children, Vol. I–III.* Grand Rapids, Michigan: Grandasia Publications, 1977. (E)

Walter, Catherine. *Genuine Articles: Authentic Reading Texts for Intermediate Students of American English.* New York: Cambridge University Press, 1986. (S/A)

Washten, Andres D. *What Happens Next? Stories to Finish for Intermediate Writers.* New York: Teachers College Press, 1978. (S/A)

Yorkey, Richard C., Richard Barrutia, Anna Uhl Chamot, Isobel Rainey De Diaz, Joas B. Gonzalez, James W. Ney, and William L. Woolf. *English for International Communication Series,* New York: American Book Company, 1977. (S/A)

Zaffran, Barbara, and David Krulik. *Hello, English, Vol. 1–6.* Lincolnwood, Illinois: National Textbook Company, 1987. (E)

VI. Workbooks

Barker, Linda. *Reach Out, Vol. 1–5*. New York: Macmillan Publishing Co., Inc., 1982. (E)

Boning, Richard A. *Getting the Facts*. Baldwin, New York: Barnell Loft, Ltd., 1977. (E/S)

____________________. *Understanding Questions*. Baldwin, New York: Dexter and Westbrook, Ltd., 1973. (E/S)

____________________. *Understanding Word Groups*. Baldwin, New York: Dexter and Westbrook, Ltd., 1973. (E/S)

Breyer, Pamela. *GrammarWork, Vol. 1–4*. New York: Regents Publishing Company, Inc., 1983. (A)

Gaines, Barbara K. *Idiomatic American English: A Step-by-Step Workbook for Learning Everyday American Expressions*. New York: Kodansha International Ltd., 1986. (E/S/A)

Gundlach, Patricia Parott, and Krenan Colton Kelsey. *Using the Phone Book*. Hayward, California: Janus Book Publishers, 1980. (E/S/A)

Jew, Wing, and Carol Tandy. *Using the Want Ads*. Hayward, California: Janus Book Publishers, 1977. (S/A)

Jew, Wing, and Robert Tong. *Janus Job Interview Kit*. Hayward, California: Janus Book Publishers, 1976. (S/A)

____________________. *Janus Job Planner*. Hayward, California: Janus Book Publishers, 1976. (S/A)

Kahn, Charles, Robert Tong, and Wing Jew. *My Job Application File*. Hayward, California: 1980. (S/A)

Letterman, Hannah, and Helen Slivka. *Word Plays: Grammar and Conversation for Beginners*. New York: Longman Inc., 1983. (A)

Livingstone, Arnold. *Janus Job Interview Guide*. Hayward, California: Janus Book Publishers, 1977. (S/A)

Petreshene, Susan A. *Mind Joggers! 5 to 15 Minute Activities That Make Kids Think*. New York: The Center for Applied Research in Education, Inc., 1986. (E)

Reeves, George. *Idioms in Action: A Key to Fluency in English*. Rowley, Massachusetts: Newbury House Publishers, Inc., 1978. (S/A)

Rickey, Jim. *Medical Language: A Survival Vocabulary*. Hayward, California: Janus Book Publishers, 1980. (E/S/A)

____________________. *Driver's License Language: A Survival Vocabulary*. Hayward, California: Janus Book Publishers, 1980. (S/A)

Roderman, Winifred Ho. *Reading Schedules*. Hayward, California: Janus Book Publishers, 1978. (E/S/A)

Rooks, George. *The Non-Stop Discussion Workbook: Problems for Intermediate and Advanced Students of English*. Rowley, Massachusetts: Newbury House Publishers, Inc., 1981. (A)

Schimpff, Jill Wagner. *Oxford Picture Dictionary of American English Workbook*. New York: Oxford University Press, 1981. (E)

Smoke, Trudy. *A Writer's Workbook: An Interactive Text for ESL Students*. New York: St. Martin's Press, 1986. (S/A)

Blackline

Masters

They've Got Your Number: Some Important Words to Know

Beginners

Directions: Write the definitions here, so you'll know them everywhere.

1. accept the charges ______________________________
2. area code ______________________________
3. busy signal ______________________________
4. collect ______________________________
5. deposit ______________________________
6. dial tone ______________________________
7. information ______________________________
8. long distance ______________________________
9. operator ______________________________
10. out of order ______________________________
11. person-to-person ______________________________
12. station-to-station ______________________________
13. wrong number ______________________________

They've Got Your Number: Some More Important Words to Know

Intermediate

Directions: Write these definitions, too. Use the words in sentences so they become part of you.

14. answering machine ______________________________

____

15. call forwarding ______________________________

____

16. call waiting ______________________________

____

17. message units ______________________________

____

18. speed calling ______________________________

____

Making Tomorrow's Career Begin Today: Some Important Words to Know

Elementary, grades 4–6

Directions: Write the definitions here, so you'll know them everywhere.

1. achieve ______________________________
____
2. amateur ______________________________
____
3. armed services ______________________________
____
4. career ______________________________
____
5. civil service ______________________________
____
6. fine arts ______________________________
____
7. future ______________________________
____
8. goals ______________________________
____
9. guardian ______________________________
____
10. hobby ______________________________
____
11. job ______________________________
____
12. laborer ______________________________
____
13. media ______________________________
____

14. profession ______________________________
____

15. professional ______________________________
____

16. public service/servant ______________________________
____

17. salespeople ______________________________
____

18. self-employed ______________________________
____

19. service careers ______________________________
____

20. skilled ______________________________
____

21. spare time/free time ______________________________
____

22. successful ______________________________
____

23. suggestions ______________________________
____

24. unskilled ______________________________
____

25. values ______________________________
____

Elementary School Survey: Grades 4–6

PART A. Answer these questions about yourself. Remember, there are no right answers or wrong answers, only truthful answers. Write your answers in the blank spaces.

1. Most of all, I like to ______________________________.
2. In my free time, I like to ______________________________.
3. I don't like to ______________________________.

Check one for each letter.

4. In the future, I would like to work:

   a. ☐ outdoors
      ☐ indoors
      ☐ It doesn't matter.

   b. ☐ with lots of people
      ☐ with a few people
      ☐ by myself

   c. ☐ in an office
      ☐ in a store
      ☐ in a house
      ☐ in a factory
      ☐ in a place where there are many kinds of jobs, for example, a hospital, newspaper, supermarket

   d. ☐ for someone
      ☐ as my own boss
      ☐ It doesn't matter.

   e. ☐ with machines, computers, etc.
      ☐ with my hands (electrician, mechanic, etc.)
      ☐ as a public servant
      ☐ as a professional (doctor, lawyer, teacher, engineer)

Write your answers in the blank spaces.

5. I am happiest when ______________________________.

6. I am saddest when ______________________________.

7. I can do these things easily:

   a. ______________________________

   b. ______________________________

   c. ______________________________

8. I have trouble with

   a. ______________________________

   b. ______________________________

   c. ______________________________

9. I value

   a. ______________________________

   b. ______________________________

   c. ______________________________

10. I am a person who primarily learns best by [check one]

    ☐ seeing ☐ hearing ☐ feeling

11. The career I've chosen can be done best by [check one]

    ☐ women

    ☐ men

    ☐ It doesn't matter.

Write your answer in the blank space.

12. The reason I feel about #11 as I do is

    ______________________________.

PART B. Write at least two answers for each question.

1. What are my goals right now?

   a. ______________________________

   b. ______________________________

2. What kind of career do I think I would be happy with in the future?

   a. ______________________________

   b. ______________________________

3. What do I think I will have to do to achieve this career?

   a. ______________________________

   b. ______________________________

4. What do I know about this career now?

   a. ______________________________

   b. ______________________________

5. Whom do I know who has this career?

   a. ______________________________

   b. ______________________________

6. If I answered #5, have I spoken to this person (these people) about the career?

   ☐ Yes ☐ No

7. If I answered "yes" to #6, what did I learn about the career from this person (these people)?

   a. ______________________________

   b. ______________________________

8. How can I find out more about this career?

   a. ______________________________

   b. ______________________________

9. Is there any reason why I should not be able to achieve this career?

☐ Yes ☐ No

10. If I answered "yes" to #9, the reasons are:

a. ______________________________

b. ______________________________

11. Three things about myself that would make me successful at the career I have chosen are: (For example, if you want to be a veterinarian, an animal doctor, one thing might be that you love animals and want to help them.)

a. ______________________________

b. ______________________________

c. ______________________________

12. Have I talked about my future with my mother, father, guardian, any member of my family?

☐ Yes ☐ No

13. If "yes," what kind of suggestions or ideas did I get from the people I spoke to?

a. ______________________________

b. ______________________________

14. What is my main interest in choosing this career?

☐ to earn a lot of money

☐ to become famous

☐ to help others

☐ to continue a family tradition

☐ other—describe ______________________________

15. What is the job outlook for this career in the next two decades?

☐ below average ☐ average ☐ above average

People Who Make it Happen

Job search: grade 4 through adult

List all the jobs you can think of at a(n):

EXAMPLE: hospital

- doctor
- nurse
- pathologist
- technicians
- dieticians
- receptionists
- security guards
- cafeteria workers

1. supermarket

2. newspaper

3. TV station

4. travel agency

5. school

6. stadium

7. farm

8. auto agency

9. military post

10. city hall

11. factory

Making Tomorrow's Career Begin Today: Some Important Words to Know

Grade 7 through adult

Directions: Write the definitions here, so you'll know them everywhere.

1. applicant ______________________________
____
2. application ______________________________
____
3. benefits ______________________________
____
4. company policy ______________________________
____
5. employee ______________________________
____
6. employer ______________________________
____
7. employment agency ______________________________
____
8. FICA ______________________________
____
9. fired ______________________________
____
10. handicaps ______________________________
____
11. hired ______________________________
____
12. interview ______________________________
____
13. interviewee ______________________________
____

14. interviewer ______________________________

____

15. laid off ______________________________

____

16. overtime ______________________________

____

17. perks ______________________________

____

18. personnel ______________________________

____

19. qualifications ______________________________

____

20. references ______________________________

____

21. résumé ______________________________

____

22. salary ______________________________

____

23. service fee ______________________________

____

24. social security ______________________________

____

25. union ______________________________

____

26. withholding tax ______________________________

____

My Career Inventory
Grade 7 through adult

Directions: Complete this inventory after you've researched a career that interests you.

Name: ______________________________

Title of Job Being Investigated: ______________________________

A. Analysis of the Career

1. Qualifications needed:

____

____

____

2. Experience needed:

____

____

3. Starting salary: ______________________________

4. Prognosis (future): ______________________________

____

5. Availability of job: ______________________________

____

6. Drawbacks/handicaps: ______________________________

____

B. Self-analysis ______________________________

1. My present qualifications and experience ______________________________

____

____

____

____

____

____

2. What I need to qualify for the career I've chosen ______________________

____

____

____

3. Can I live on the salary offered? ______________________

4. Is the job worth it? ______________________

5. Am I willing to relocate, if necessary? ______________________

6. Is there prejudice to be faced in this career with regard to sex, religion, race, age? Can I cope with it? ______________________

____

____

7. Do I have the stamina, determination, "equipment" to deal with the emotional, physical, and mental demands of this career? ______________________

____

____

8a. Why do I want this career? How can I achieve it now that I've decided I am suited for it? ______________________

____

____

8b. What have I learned about myself? Where do I go from here, now that I know this career is not really what I want right now? ______________________

____

____

Reference Materials Used:

Title: ______________	Title: ______________
Author/Publisher: ______________	Author/Publisher: ______________
Date of Publication: ______________	Date of Publication: ______________

Application for Employment

Grade 7 through adult

Directions: Complete this application. Because this is *practice* in filling out an application, you may "create" information about yourself. (Remember: you must be truthful and accurate when filling out the real thing.)

RAINBOW INDUSTRIES

Please print clearly.

Date: ______________

GENERAL INFORMATION

Name: ______________________________

Address: ______________________________

____

Phone: (___) ___-______ Social Security No.: ______-______-______

Languages speak: ______________ Languages write: ______________

Position Desired: ______________ Salary Expected: ______________

EDUCATIONAL BACKGROUND

Name of High School ______________________________

Address ______________________________

Dates Attended ______________ Diploma/Degree/Certificate Earned ______________

Name of Vocational School ______________________________

Address ______________________________

Dates Attended ______________ Diploma/Degree/Certificate Earned ______________

Name of College ______________________________

Address ______________________________

Dates Attended ______________ Diploma/Degree/Certificate Earned ______________

Other Training ______________________________

Address ______________________________

Dates Attended ______________ Diploma/Degree/Certificate Earned ______________

EMPLOYMENT RECORD

List all previous jobs in order of *last job first.*

1. Company ____________________ Address ____________________

   Title/Type of Work ____________________ Salary __________

   From ______ To ______ Reason Left: ____________________

2. Company ____________________ Address ____________________

   Title/Type of Work ____________________ Salary __________

   From ______ To ______ Reason Left: ____________________

3. Company ____________________ Address ____________________

   Title/Type of Work ____________________ Salary __________

   From ______ To ______ Reason Left: ____________________

4. Company ____________________ Address ____________________

   Title/Type of Work ____________________ Salary __________

   From ______ To ______ Reason Left: ____________________

REFERENCES

These individuals will be contacted for information about your character, ability, and potential. *(No relatives, please.)*

Name ______________________________

Address ______________________________

Phone No. (___) - ______________________________

Occupation ______________________________

How long have you known this person? ____________________

Name ______________________________

Address ______________________________

Phone No. (___) - ______________________________

Occupation ______________________________

How long have you known this person? ____________________

____

Applicant's Signature

Making the System Work for You: Some Important Words to Know

Directions: Write the definitions here, so you'll know them everywhere.

1. absentee landlord ______________________________
____
2. addict ______________________________
____
3. apartment ______________________________
____
4. attic ______________________________
____
5. corporation ______________________________
____
6. deposit ______________________________
____
7. derelict ______________________________
____
8. eviction ______________________________
____
9. exterminator ______________________________
____
10. flat ______________________________
____
11. fluorescent ______________________________
____
12. hazards ______________________________
____
13. insurance ______________________________
____

14. interest ____

____

15. landlord ____

____

16. lease ____

____

17. liability ____

____

18. litter ____

____

19. mortgage ____

____

20. plumbing ____

____

21. receipt ____

____

22. rent ____

____

23. responsibilities ____

____

24. rights ____

____

25. rodents ____

____

26. run-down ____

____

27. security ______________________________

____

28. slumlord ______________________________

____

29. sublet ______________________________

____

30. superintendent ______________________________

____

31. tenant ______________________________

____

32. tenement ______________________________

____

Housing Inspection for (Address of Premises)

Directions: Make a careful inspection of the place where you live. Check each item honestly, using the back of the page to continue your comments, if necessary.

Item	Satisfactory	Unsatisfactory	Comments
I. Exterior			
A. Sidewalks, fences, immediate surroundings			
1. free from litter	____	____	____________
2. in good repair	____	____	____________
3. sufficiently well lit where indicated	____	____	____________
B. Outside brick, paint, and so forth in good repair	____	____	____________
C. Doors, windows properly secured: locks in good working order	____	____	____________
D. Garbage disposal areas:			
1. sufficient covered areas for disposal	____	____	____________
2. area clean and free from infestation	____	____	____________
3. adequate garbage collection to avoid overflow	____	____	____________
II. Interiors			
A. Communal hallways, stairwells, areas			
1. properly lit	____	____	____________
2. free from garbage and litter	____	____	____________
B. Paint in good repair	____	____	____________
C. Mailboxes properly secured	____	____	____________
D. Exits not blocked by carriages, bicycles, litter	____	____	____________
E. Fire escapes working properly and free from litter	____	____	____________
F. Easy access to fire escapes, all exits (special stress in this area is necessary because of frequency of fires in many older buildings)	____	____	____________
III. Individual premises			
A. Sufficient heat and hot water	____	____	____________
B. Plumbing in good order	____	____	____________
C. Sufficient electrical outlets	____	____	____________
D. Outlets working properly	____	____	____________
E. Stove in good working condition	____	____	____________
F. Paint in good repair: no peeling, no lead paints, no holes or leaks	____	____	____________
G. Landlord abides by state law (e.g., in some states, tenant is entitled to free paint job every three years).	____	____	____________
H. Apartment is free from infestation: adequate extermination control (in New Jersey, a new tenant in an apartment is entitled to a paint job, free of charge, extermination service, and a municipal inspection before moving into the apartment, that is, as of this printing).	____	____	____________

Preparing Consumer Education Units: Some Important Words to Know

Directions: Write the definitions here, so you'll know them everywhere.

1. consumer ______________________________
2. comparison shopping ______________________________
3. "caveat emptor" ______________________________
4. Better Business Bureau ______________________________
5. Office of Consumer Affairs ______________________________
6. Legal Aid Society ______________________________
7. Small Claims Court ______________________________
8. defendant ______________________________
9. plaintiff ______________________________
10. collection agency ______________________________
11. loan company (finance company) ______________________________
12. loan shark ______________________________
13. interest ______________________________

14. usury ______________________________

____

15. illegal ______________________________

____

16. swindle ______________________________

____

17. bait and switch ______________________________

____

18. chain referral ______________________________

____

19. consolidation loan ______________________________

____

20. credit certificates ______________________________

____

21. advertisements ______________________________

____

22. commercials ______________________________

____

23. degrees of truth (direct lies vs. indirect lies) ______________________________

____

24. lay-away plan ______________________________

____

25. installment plan ______________________________

____

26. charge ______________________________

____

27. down payment ______________________________

____

28. balance ______________________________

____

29. bargain ______________________________

____

30. installed ______________________________

____

31. warranty, guarantee ______________________________

____

32. contract ______________________________

____

33. bill ______________________________

____

34. truth-in-lending ______________________________

____

35. shrink ______________________________

____

36. faded ______________________________

____

37. summons ______________________________

____

38. cheated ______________________________

____

39. risk ______________________________

____

40. fair price ____

____

41. manufacturer ____

____

42. limitations ____

____

43. sales trap ____

____

44. unsolicited ____

____

45. goods ____

____

46. hard sell vs. soft sell ____

____

47. sales pitch ____

____

Writing Practice: Sample Exercise 1

Intermediate

Directions: Read the paragraph below carefully. Be sure you understand it. Then, change *Henry* and *he* to *I* and rewrite the paragraph in the space provided, telling about yourself. Use the "Oh, Henry!" paragraph as a model when writing about yourself. When you have finished rewriting the exercise, go back and make sure that you have changed everything that needs to be changed.

"Oh, Henry!"

Henry hates baseball. He doesn't like football either. He loves to dance, sing, and write songs. He'd rather play the drums than play soccer. He wants to be an entertainer. He doesn't enjoy sitting in the cold and cheering for people who run up and down a field with a pigskin in their hands. He considers it stupid to try to hit a ball with a bat. In fact, he likes bats that fly and thinks pigskin belongs on pigs. That Henry is something else!

"Oh, Henry!"

____

____

____

____

____

____

____

____

____

____

____

____

____

____

____

Writing Practice: Sample Exercise 2

Advanced

Directions: Read the paragraph below carefully. Be sure you understand it. Then, change *my name* to *her name* and rewrite the paragraph in the space provided. When you have finished rewriting the exercise, go back and make sure that you have changed everything that needs to be changed.

"Pat at Bat"

My name is Pat. Although I'm still in junior high school, I have decided on my career. I dream that some day I will go to college and become a lawyer. I want to help people. Frankly, I will be a good lawyer. I always try my best. I love sports! Baseball is my favorite sport. My ambition is to be a lawyer for professional athletes. My job would be to represent them at contract time and whenever else I can help them.

"Pat at Bat"

For the Teacher: Unit Evaluation Form

Teacher's Name: ______________________ Class/Grade: __________/__________

Date: ______________________ Proficiency level(s): ______________________

Name of Unit: ______________________ Overall Evaluation: ______________________

DIRECTIONS: A. Briefly describe the unit as follows:

1. Purpose(s): ____

2. Goal(s): ____

3. Procedure: ____

4. Outcomes: ____

5. Method(s) of Evaluation: ____

B. Evaluate the unit's overall success, using the following scale:

1 = Yes, definitely

2 = Most of the time

3 = Some of the time

4 = Not really

__________ Was it worth the time and effort?

__________ Did you reach at least *some* of your students?

__________ Did all of you have fun?

__________ Have the students' self-awareness and confidence increased?

__________ Did the project lend itself to the natural use of language?

__________ Was the response from others, *e.g.*, parents, community members, classmates, positive?

C. Would you do this unit again with another group? Check only one.

__________ Yes, as is.

__________ Yes, but with a few changes.

__________ Yes, but with several changes.

__________ No, never again.

D. OVERALL UNIT RATING: Circle one.

1. Excellent unit
2. Very good unit
3. Good unit
4. Fair unit
5. Poor unit

E. Additional Comments: ____

____